Christmas
Crafts
and
Activities

Gospel Light

How to make clean copies from this book

You may make copies of portions of this book with a clean conscience if:

✦ you (or someone in your organization) are the original purchaser;

✦ you are using the copies you make for a noncommercial purpose (such as teaching or promoting a ministry) within your church or organization;

✦ you follow the instructions provided in this book.

However, it is ILLEGAL for you to make copies if:

✦ you are using the material to promote, advertise or sell a product or service other than for ministry fund-raising;

✦ you are using the material in or on a product for sale; or

✦ you or your organization are **not** the original purchaser of this book.

By following these guidelines you help us keep our products affordable. Thank you.

Gospel Light

Contents

GAMES 85
Game Tips..86

Lower Elementary

Upper Elementary

ACTIVITIES 101
Activity Tips...102

Early Childhood

Introduction

What's a parent or teacher to do with all the extra energy children have at Christmas? Here's the help you need—ideas for sharing special times with your child, for providing unique experiences for your child and his or her friends, or for supplementing or creating special programs for December churchtime, for a mid-week Advent program, for a kids' club or for a homeschool setting.

How to Get the Most Out of This Book

First, look through all the sections ("Crafts," "Games," "Activities," "Stories" and "Snacks") to acquaint yourself with all the ideas you now have at your fingertips.

- Each section begins with helpful tips to make your efforts in that area easier and more effective.
- Each craft, game and activity is labeled with the appropriate age level and contains a complete list of needed materials. Many of them include conversation guides to help you share the true message of Christmas with children.
- Four exciting installments of the Christmas story complete with discussion questions and Bible memory verses and delicious, easy-to-prepare snacks round out the resources assembled for you.

If you are leading a large group of children, be sure to plan your program and choose your activities well in advance. That will give you time to recruit any helpers and gather the materials you'll need.

We suggest these schedule options:

Early Childhood (Ages 2-5)
60 minutes

Activities (2-3): 30 minutes
Bible Story: 5 minutes
Snack: 10 minutes
Craft: 15 minutes

90 minutes

Activities (3-4): 40 minutes
Bible Story: 5 minutes
Free Play: 20 minutes
Snack: 10 minutes
Craft: 15 minutes

Elementary (Grades 1-6)
60 minutes

Activity: 15 minutes
Bible Story: 15 minutes
Game or Snack: 15 minutes
Craft: 15 minutes

90 minutes

Activity: 20 minutes
Bible Story: 20 minutes
Game or Snack: 20 minutes
Craft: 30 minutes

Once you have these basics in hand, we hope you will be inspired to add your own creative ideas. There is no time like Christmas to help a child discover and relish the truth, wonder and joy embodied in the birth of God's Son, Jesus.

Have a joyous Christmas—and may God bless your endeavors with kids!

Parent Tips: Keeping Perspective

Christmas! The word itself stirs feelings of extraordinary excitement—and rightly so. Everywhere there are reminders of the holiday season, but let's be sure our children know what the excitement is really about.

How can parents help a young child realize that Christmas is a celebration of gratitude to God for His wonderful gift of love? Here are suggestions for ways you can make the biblical and spiritual aspects of Christmas meaningful and attractive to your child.

Help your child know the simple facts of Jesus' birth as they are recorded in Scripture.

- Read the story of the first Christmas to your child from Bible storybooks or from an easy-to-understand version of the Bible.
- Visit your Christian bookstore and choose books and/or videos that will appeal to your child.

Help your child feel that Jesus is God's best gift of love.

- Remember that much of a child's response is a reflection of the attitudes he or she sees at home. Nurture feelings of joy, love and thankfulness in your child.
- Avoid (as much as possible) the hurry and busyness of Christmas that make a young child feel alone or "left out."
- In the presence of your child, give thanks to God for Jesus.
- Include your child in family plans for expressing love to Jesus by caring and loving others. (Make cookies for elderly relatives, shut-ins, etc. Send cards to friends. Plan surprises for grandparents. Take canned foods or personal care items to a rescue mission, etc.)

Help your child express joy, excitement and feelings of love.

- Include your child in making Christmas decorations, foods, gifts and cards for family members and friends.
- Show gladness to your child as you sing the songs of Christmas. Find out and learn the songs your child is learning at church so you can sing them together at home.
- Be sensitive to moments when it is natural to talk about God and encourage your child to talk to God with thanks and praise.

Keep Santa in the proper perspective.

- Avoid referring to Santa as a real person. (Explain that Santa legends may be based on a real St. Nicholas who loved God and gave generously to the poor. A useful phrase is "Talking about Santa is fun, and it's even better to talk about Jesus who loves us all year long.")
- Avoid using such Santa-emphasizing phrases as "What do you want Santa to bring you for Christmas?" and "Be good for Santa."
- When your child wants to talk about Santa Claus, listen attentively. Then say, "That's fun. Santa's a happy pretend fellow."

- Keep the meaning of Christmas clear by frequently commenting, "Christmas is a happy time because it is Jesus' birthday."
- Bake a birthday cake for Jesus. Children will understand that because Christmas is Jesus' birthday there should be a cake! Sing "Happy Birthday" to Jesus and plan together what your family can give Him for a gift of love.

(This and other helpful articles for parents and teachers can be found in the reproducible *Sunday School Smart Pages* by Gospel Light.)

Crafts

Craft Tips

Few things spark a child's imagination like working with a craft. When children are cutting, gluing, pasting, drawing or shaping, they are using their imaginations to picture and better understand a truth or an idea. Many children think more clearly when they are doing something than when they are sitting still. While they are working, different parts of their minds are engaged in thinking and understanding.

What can you do to make sure craft time is successful and fun for children?

- Encourage creativity in each child! Remember that the process of creating is just as important as the final product.
- Choose projects that are appropriate for the skill level of the children you are dealing with.
- Show an interest in the unique way each child approaches a project. Treat each child's product as a "masterpiece!"

Helpful Hints for Using Crafts with Young Children

Folding

1. Before giving paper to child, prefold paper as needed; then open it back up. Paper will then fold easily along the prefolded lines when child refolds it.

2. Score the line to be folded by placing a ruler on the line. Then draw a ballpoint pen with no ink in it along the ruler's edge. The line will fold easily into place.

3. Hold the corners of the paper in position to be folded. Tell the child to "press and rub" where he or she wants to fold it.

Taping

1. An easy solution for the problems of taping is to use double-sided tape whenever appropriate. Lay the tape down on the paper where it is needed. Child attaches the item that needs to be taped.

2. If double-sided tape is not available or is not appropriate, place a piece of tape lightly on the page where indicated. Child rubs on tape to attach it securely to paper.

Cutting

1. Cutting with scissors is one of the most difficult tasks for any young child to master. Consider purchasing "training scissors" (available at educational supply stores) to assist in teaching a child how to cut.

2. If you have a large group of children, have available two or three pairs of left-handed scissors (also available at educational supply stores). All scissors should be approximately 4 inches (10 cm) long and should have blunt ends.

3. Hold paper tightly at ends or sides while child cuts.

4. Begin to cut paper for child to follow. Child follows cut you have begun.

5. Draw simple lines outside actual cut lines for the child to follow. This will help a child cut close to the desired shape—though it will not be exact.

6. Provide scrap paper for child to practice cutting.

Gluing

1. Have child use a glue bottle to apply a spot of glue to a large sheet of paper; then he or she presses a smaller piece of paper onto glued area.

2. Provide a glue stick for the child to use (available at variety stores). Take off cap and roll up glue for child. Child "colors" with glue stick over desired area.

3. Pour glue into a shallow container. Thin slightly by adding a small amount of water. Child uses paintbrush to spread glue over desired area. This idea works well when a large surface needs to be glued.

4. To glue a smaller surface, pour a small amount of glue into a shallow container. Give child a cotton swab. Child dips the swab into the glue and rubs on desired area.

5. When using glue bottles, buy the smallest bottles for children to use. Refill small bottles

from a large bottle. (a) Adjust top to limit amount of glue that comes out. (b) Instruct child to put "tiny dots of glue" on paper. (c) Clean off and tightly close top of bottle when finished.

Remember not to expect perfection. Accept all attempts at accomplishing the task. Specific and honest praise will encourage the child to attempt the task again!

(These and other helpful hints for parents and teachers can be found in the reproducible *Sunday School Smart Pages* by Gospel Light.)

Crayon Stars

Materials: White crayon, one sheet of white paper for each child, dark blue thinned liquid tempera paint, paintbrushes, paint smocks (or old shirts), newspapers.

Preparation: Use white crayon to draw and color several stars on each paper. Make one star larger than others. Apply crayon heavily for best results. Cover work area with newspapers.

Procedure: Put a smock on each child. Child brushes paint over paper. Paint will "resist" crayoned areas and allow stars to show through.

When can you see stars like these in the sky? How many stars do you think are in the sky? Who made all the stars? At Christmastime we hear about a special star God put in the sky the night Jesus was born. Some wise men followed that star. When they found Jesus, they worshiped Him and gave Him gifts.

Christmas Folder

Materials: Sponges, scissors, ruler, spring-type clothespins, red and green liquid tempera paint, shallow pans, felt pens, one sheet of white construction paper for each child, newspapers, paint smocks (or old shirts).

Preparation: Cut wet sponges into 2-inch (5-cm) pieces. Attach clothespins to sponges. Pour paint into pans. Fold and letter each paper as shown. Cover work area with newspapers.

Procedure: Put a smock on each child. Child decorates blank side of paper with sponge painting. When dry, fold in half with lettering inside.

These words tell us that God sent us His Son, Jesus. We are glad that Jesus was born!

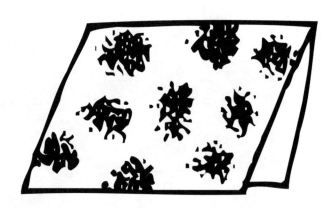

Patchwork Poster

Materials: One sheet of white construction paper for each child, felt pens, several patterns of Christmas wrapping paper, ruler, scissors, glue.

Preparation: Letter the word "LOVE" in block letters on each sheet of white construction paper. Cut wrapping paper into 1-inch (2.5-cm) squares.

Procedure: Show one of the lettered sheets of paper. Point out the word and explain that we can celebrate Christmas by showing love to others. Children glue squares of wrapping paper inside block letters. While children are working ask, **How has someone shown love to you during this Christmas season? How can you show love to others?**

Christmas Cards

Materials: 9×12-inch (22.5×30-cm) red and green construction paper, felt pen, red and green curling ribbon, scissors, seasonal stickers, glue or tape; optional—additional decorating items (glitter crayons, squares of seasonal wrapping paper, etc.).

Preparation: Prefold each sheet of paper in half to make a card. Letter cards as shown in sketch a. Cut ribbon into 6-inch (15-cm) lengths, several for each card. Slightly curl ribbon with scissors' edge.

Procedure: Child folds card and decorates the front of the card by adding stickers and gluing or taping ribbon curls. (Optional: Child uses additional items to decorate front of card.) Ask each child to name someone to whom he or she would like to send the card. Write names on card fronts as shown in sketch b. Help children sign their names.

Some people send special cards to their friends and families at Christmastime. Our cards tell that Jesus was born. I'm thankful for the good news that Jesus was born!

Star Rubbings

Materials: Star Rubbings Patterns, light-weight cardboard, pencil, scissors, dark blue construction paper, unwrapped yellow crayons; optional—glue, shallow box, glitter.

Preparation: Use patterns to trace four or five cardboard star shapes and then cut them out. Prefold one or two sheets of construction paper in half for each child.

Procedure: Demonstrate how to place star shape inside folded paper and rub side of crayon across the paper until the star shape shows. Child folds paper and completes several star rubbings. Show children how to move the star shape to make more than one rubbing on each sheet of paper. (Optional: After completing the rubbing, help children spread glue onto stars. Place star in a shallow box. Children sprinkle glitter onto glue. Help them shake off excess glitter.)

After Jesus was born, some wise men saw a bright star shining in the sky. The wise men packed special gifts and started on a long trip to find God's Son, Jesus. They followed the star for a long time, looking for Jesus. When the wise men found Jesus, they were happy! The wise men were thankful for the star that led them to Jesus. I'm thankful, too.

Crafts • **Early Childhood**
Star Rubbings Patterns

Christmas Crafts and Activities © 1998 by Gospel Light. Permission to photocopy granted.

Nature Craft

Materials: Variety of small seasonal nature items (pinecones, sprigs of holly, fir, spruce and/or pine), white construction paper, glue; optional—paper bags, one or more magnifying glasses.

Preparation: Remove any berries from sprigs.

Procedure: Children glue nature items onto paper. (Optional: If appropriate in your area, take children on a walk outdoors to collect nature items listed above. Give each child a paper bag in which to place items.) As children examine the items, talk with them about things for which they may thank God. (Optional: Children use magnifying glasses to examine items.) Ask child to tell something he or she is thankful for. Letter "I thank God for _____." on child's paper.

God has made so many beautiful things. I'm glad God gave us (green trees) to look at. We can use (branches like these) to decorate at Christmas. Christmas is a wonderful time to thank God for the beautiful things He made.

Glitter Star

Materials: Glitter Star Pattern, one sheet of white construction paper for each child, pencil, newspaper, glue, cotton swabs, gold and/or silver glitter; optional—scissors, hole punch, string, tacks or masking tape.

Preparation: Trace a Glitter Star Pattern on each sheet of paper. Cover work area with newspaper.

Procedure: Children spread glue on stars with cotton swabs and then sprinkle glitter over glue. (Optional: Cut out star. Punch hole at top of each star. Tie string and hang from ceiling.)

God helped some wise men follow a very special star to find Jesus after He was born. The wise men thanked God for the special star that helped them find Jesus. When you see your glitter star, you can thank God just like the wise men did.

Celebration Bells

Materials: Egg cartons, scissors, lightweight collage materials (fabric and paper scraps, ribbon, stickers, etc.), glue, red and green chenille wire, small jingle bells.

Preparation: Use scissors to punch a small hole through the top of each egg carton segment. Cut segments apart. Prepare several segments for each child.

Procedure: For each bell, children glue collage materials to carton segment. Then they thread a jingle bell onto a chenille wire, twisting the end of the wire several times to secure bell. Child pushes other end of chenille wire through hole in carton segment, looping and twisting the end of the wire to form a hanger. Children shake bells in praise as they sing a Christmas song. (Optional: While children work, make a bell cluster for your door. Make five or six bells, twisting ends together. Tape cluster to door.)

Today we're making bells to help us celebrate Jesus' birth. These bells will help us make happy music. We are happy because God sent His Son, Jesus.

chenille wire

bell

bell inside

Advent Chains

Materials: Red and green construction paper, paper cutter, a December calendar, tape, crayons, seasonal and nativity scene stickers, small unbreakable Christmas ornaments.

Preparation: Use paper cutter to cut construction paper into 2×12-inch (5×30-cm) strips. Cut enough strips so that every child may make a chain representing each day from today until Christmas day.

Procedure: Show December calendar and help children count days until Christmas. Each child decorates his or her strips and tapes them together to form a chain. Place nativity scene stickers on December 25th loops of all chains. (If you combine all chains into a large one, hang small Christmas ornaments from some of the loops.)

I'm glad Christmas will be here soon! Christmas shows us how much God loves us. God loves us so much that He sent His Son, Jesus. When you get home, ask someone in your family to help you hang your Christmas chain. You can tear off one loop each day until Christmas comes.

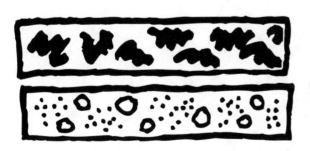

Tape

Christmas Trees

Materials: Christmas Tree Pattern, pencil, one sheet of green construction paper for each child, scissors, glue, salt in salt shakers, shallow pan.

Preparation: Trace a Christmas Tree Pattern on each sheet of construction paper.

Procedure: Each child selects a tree, cuts it out and then squeezes or spreads glue on the tree to form decorations (stars, triangles, balls, etc.). Children shake salt onto glued areas. Help them shake off excess salt into shallow pan.

Do you have a Christmas tree at your house this year? What are your favorite decorations on your tree? All the lights and the pretty colors on the tree help me remember that Christmas is Jesus' birthday. When we look at our Christmas trees, we can say, "Happy Birthday, Jesus!"

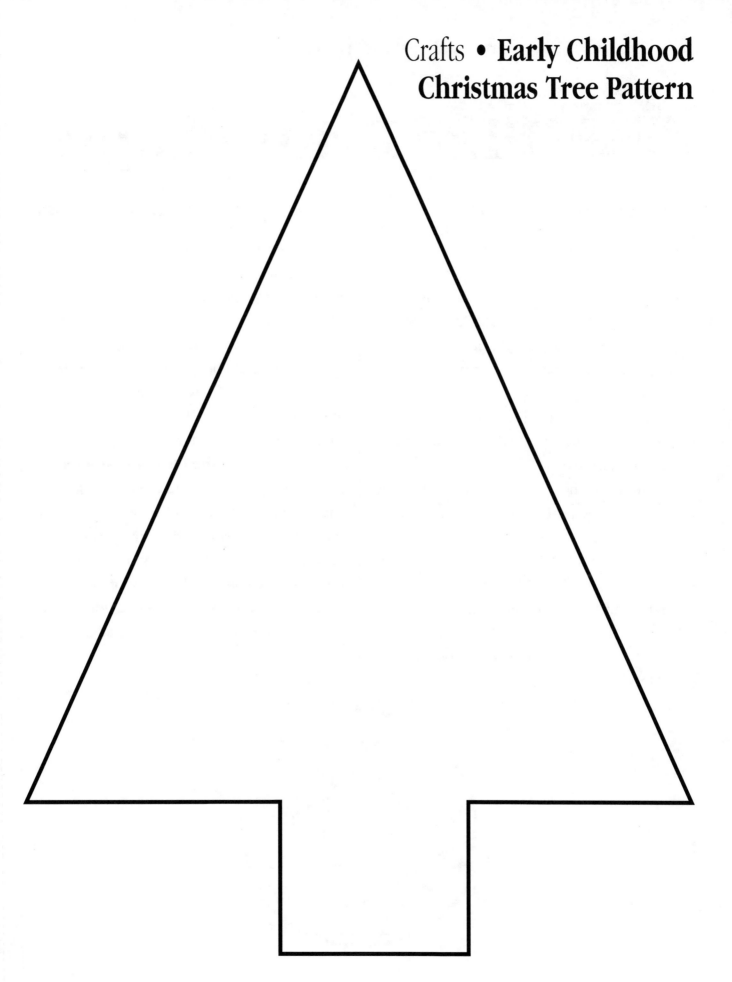

Pine Print Plaque

Materials: Saucepan, stove, wooden spoon, materials for cornstarch dough (1 cup cornstarch, 2 cups baking soda, 1 1/4 cups water), waxed paper, winter nature items (such as small pine boughs, pinecones, twigs); optional—pencil, string or narrow ribbon.

Preparation: Mix the ingredients for dough in saucepan. Cook over medium heat until mixture thickens. Cool and then flatten dough into rounds, one for each child. Place rounds between sheets of waxed paper to keep from drying out.

Procedure: Children press nature items into the dough to make impressions and then carefully lift items off. Impressions may be saved or dough may be reshaped and reused. (Optional: To preserve impressions as small plaques or ornaments, use a pencil to make two holes near the edge of the dough about a pencil's width apart; let plaques dry for about five days. When dry, add string or ribbon for hanging.)

Encourage children to notice the details of the impressions they are making. Talk about how each item shows God's loving care for His world and the creatures in it.

God cares for the birds and squirrels by making food for them and giving them places to live. God cares for you, too. Once you were a tiny baby. Did you stay a baby? No! God gave you a family to take care of you and help you grow big and strong. Christmastime is a good time to thank God for His wonderful care.

Tissue Wreaths

Materials: One 7-inch (17.5-cm) white paper plate for each child, scissors, ruler, green tissue paper, red yarn, hole punch, red construction paper, newspaper, glue.

Preparation: Cut the center from each paper plate to make a wreath shape. Cut tissue paper into 7-inch (17.5-cm) squares. Cut yarn into 18-inch (45-cm) lengths. Punch two holes near plate edge. Punch out paper-circle "berries" from red construction paper; make several "berries" for each child. Cover work area with newspaper.

Procedure: Children crumple tissue squares and glue them to the plate rims. Children use dots of glue to put "berries" onto the wreaths and then thread yarn through holes at tope of plates. Tie yarn in a bow. As children work, let them share their excitement over the holidays with you.

Your family will be glad to see your decoration! What do you get excited about at Christmas time? Christmas is a happy time! Christmas is when we celebrate Jesus' birthday.

Christmas Mittens

Materials: Construction paper, felt pen, Christmas stickers, fabric or construction paper scraps, glue, scissors, hole punch, yarn or string; optional—crayons, cotton balls.

Procedure: Child places both hands—palms down, fingers slightly apart—on construction paper. Draw a mitten outline around hands. (See sketch a.) Child decorates mittens with stickers and/or fabric or paper scraps. Cut out mittens. Punch a hole at the bottom of each mitten and connect with string or yarn. (See sketch b.) Letter child's name on back of one of his or her mittens. (Optional: In addition to making mittens, draw a hat outline for children to decorate with paper or fabric scraps or to color with crayons. Provide cotton balls for children to glue to top of hats as pom-poms.)

These mittens make me feel warm. Mary kept baby Jesus warm on the night He was born. She wrapped Him up and put Him in a soft bed. Who helps you stay warm on a cold night? God loves you and gave you a family to take good care of you. Christmas is a good time to say, "Thank You, God, for my family."

a.

b.

Christmas Collage

Materials: Scissors, assorted collage materials (Christmas wrapping paper, used Christmas cards fronts, net, fabric, ribbon, red and green chenille wires, small discarded wrapping decorations), glue, 9x12-inch (22.5x30-cm) sheet of construction paper or cardboard for each child.

Preparation: Cut collage materials into a variety of manageable shapes.

Procedure: To make collage, child selects, arranges and pastes various materials on paper in a way that is pleasing to him or her. There is no right or wrong way to make a collage. As children work, try to relate the colors, shapes and textures of the materials to the message of Christmas.

The shiny gold paper looks like our pretty Christmas decorations. When we decorate our homes, it looks like we're going to have a party! Whose birthday is it? Christmas is Jesus' birthday, and we are glad!

Christmas Circle Ornaments

Materials: Red and green construction paper, drawing compass, ruler, pencil, scissors, ribbon or yarn, Christmas stickers, tape, hole punch.

Preparation: Cut 4-inch (10-cm) circles from construction paper—one red and one green for each child. In each circle, cut a 2-inch (5-cm) slit as shown. Cut ribbon or yarn into 8-inch (20-cm) lengths—one for each child.

Procedure: To make ornament, child slips a red circle into a green one. Child adds stickers for decoration. Adjust circles to right angles and secure with tape. Punch hole in top. Thread ribbon through hole and tie ends for hanger.

This ornament is shaped like the world! It reminds me of a verse in our Bible. Our Bible says that God loves everyone in the world and sent us His Son, Jesus. Where will you hang your ornament? When you look at your ornament, you can think of how much God loves you!

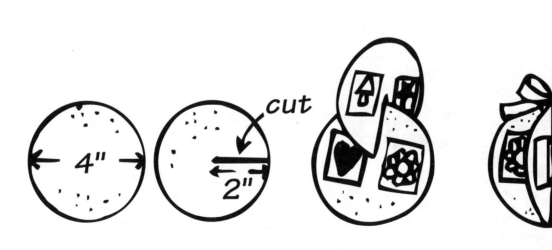

Christmas Crafts and Activities © 1998 by Gospel Light. Permission to photocopy granted.

Doorknob Hanger

Materials: Doorknob Hanger Pattern, red and green felt, pen, scissors, Christmas stickers or red and green yarn, glue.

Preparation: Trace Doorknob Hanger Pattern onto felt, one for each child. Cut out. Cut slits as shown so hanger will slip easily over doorknob.

Procedure: Children decorate doorknob hanger by pressing stickers or gluing yarn pieces to felt. Ask a child to demonstrate use of doorknob hanger.

Do you have Christmas decorations at your house? Your family will be glad to see your pretty doorknob hanger. Whenever you open or close your door, you can remember that Christmas is when Jesus was born.

Crafts • Early Childhood
Doorknob Hanger Pattern

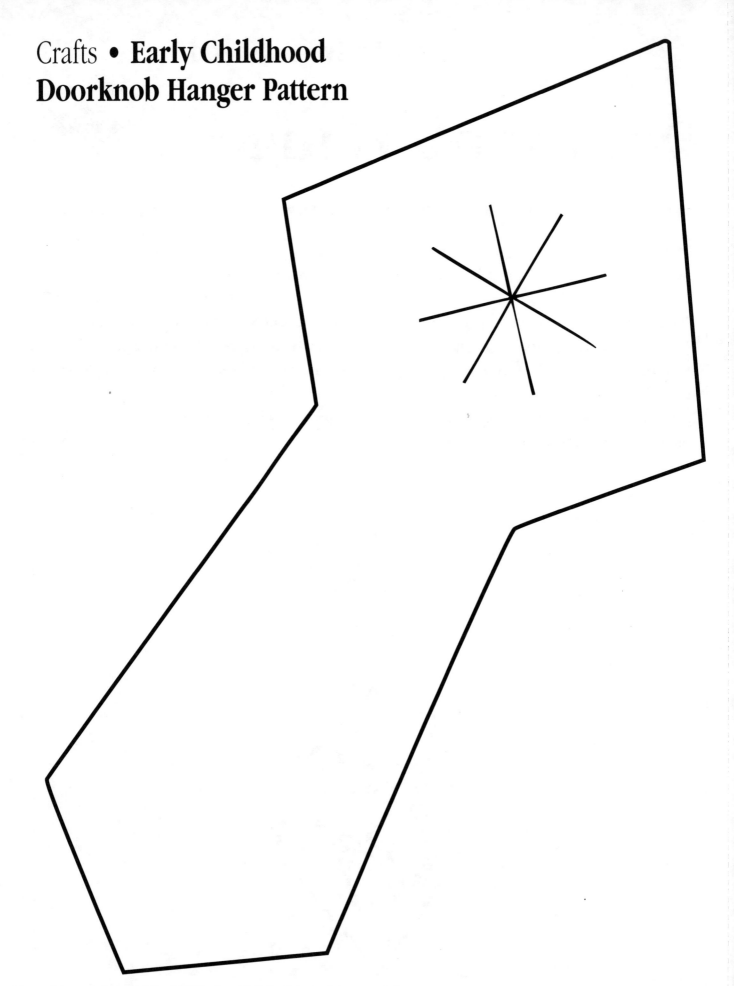

Telling the Good News

Materials: Telling the Good News Figure Patterns, photocopier, paper or card stock, crayons, scissors, paper clips.

Preparation: Photocopy a set of the patterns for each child.

Procedure: Children color and cut out figures. Help them fold the figures where indicated to make them stand. Paper clip figures together for children to take home.

All of these people heard the good news in our Christmas story! The angel told Mary that she was going to have a baby who would be God's Son, Jesus. Mary told the good news to her friend Elizabeth. An angel told Joseph that Jesus was going to be born, too. Everyone was so happy to hear the good news! What do you like to do when you hear good news? What good news can we tell our friends about Christmas?

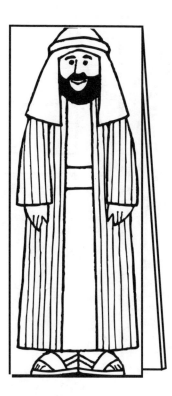

Tube Angels

Materials: Scissors, white tissue paper, yellow yarn, ruler, drawing compass, gold foil, newspaper, tape, glue, glue brushes, gold-colored gummed stars. For each child—toilet tissue or paper towel tube 4 1/2 inches (11.25 cm) long, 2-inch (5-cm) Styrofoam ball, white fluted coffee filter.

Preparation: Assemble a sample angel. Cut tissue paper to cover each tube. Cut yarn in 6-inch (15-cm) lengths for hair. Cut 2-inch (5-cm) circles from gold foil. Cut filters in half. Cover work area with newspaper.

Procedure: Let children do as much of this project as possible. Tape tissue paper to tube and stand tube on one end. Brush glue along top edge of tube and attach Styrofoam ball for head. Spread glue on top of head and place lengths of yarn for hair. For halo, glue foil circle to back of head so that gold color shows in the front. For wings, spread glue on flat edges of filter halves and attach to back of body. Stick stars on body front.

Angels up in the night sky told some shepherds about Jesus' birth. The shepherds hurried to see baby Jesus. They were very glad about the news and told everyone they met that God's Son, Jesus, was born. We are glad that Jesus was born, too! We can sing about Jesus just like the angels did!

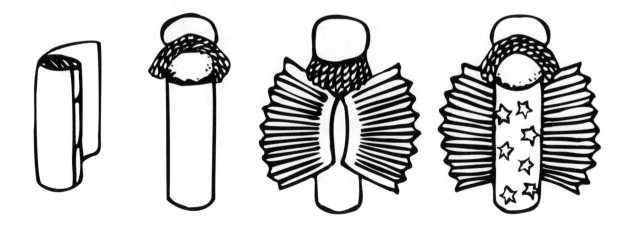

Christmas Messages

Materials: Used Christmas cards, scissors, red or green construction paper, butcher paper, felt pens, white, red or green yarn, glue.

Preparation: Cut out pictures from cards. Prefold construction paper in half. Make a sample card following directions below.

Procedure: Ask children to name something they would like to tell a friend about Christmas. Write children's ideas on butcher paper. If children need help, ask leading questions or suggest answers. (God sent Jesus. God loves us. Angels told the shepherds good news.) Each child chooses the message he or she wants to write on a card. Give each child a piece of construction paper. Children fold papers in half and glue a picture to the front of the card. Place a thin line of glue around the edge of the card and have children press yarn on the glue line. Help children write their Christmas messages on the inside of their cards and sign their names.

When you give your card to someone you can tell them, "Christmas means God loves you."

Christmas Crafts and Activities © 1998 by Gospel Light. Permission to photocopy granted.

Salt/Flour Dough "Cookies"

Materials: Dough ingredients for the recipe you choose, measuring cups and spoons, plastic bags, mixing bowl and spoon, toy rolling pins, waxed paper, Christmas cookie cutters.

Preparation: Measure ingredients into plastic bags.

Procedure: Children name and mix dough ingredients. (You will need to complete mixing.) Children pretend to make Christmas cookies by using toy rolling pins to flatten small balls of dough on waxed paper. Demonstrate using cookie cutter. Let children make cookies and pretend to share them with each other.

Why do we make cookies and have pretty decorations at Christmas time? Christmas is when we celebrate Jesus' birthday! We can celebrate Jesus' birthday by sharing with each other.

Recipe No. 1

2 parts flour

1 part salt

1 tablespoon alum

Add water and dry tempera to achieve desired consistency and color.

Recipe No. 2

4 cups flour

2 cups salt

1/4 cup salad oil

1/8 cup soap flakes

2 cups water

1/8 cup alum

food coloring

Recipe No. 3

1 1/2 cups flour

1 cup cornstarch

1 cup salt

1 cup warm water

food coloring

Recipe No. 4 (cooked)

1 cup flour

1 cup water

1/2 cup salt

1 tablespoon cooking oil

2 teaspoons cream of tartar

food coloring

Cook until consistency of mashed potatoes. Do not boil. Knead until cool.

For all recipes: If dough is sticky, dust with flour. If dough is stiff, add water. All doughs need to be stored in airtight containers. Recipe No. 3 hardens nicely and can be painted if "cookies" are to be preserved.

Christmas Tree Birthday Card

Materials: Green and white construction paper, felt pen, Christmas Tree Birthday Card Pattern, scissors, glue, glue brushes, gummed or self-adhesive stars in different sizes, a variety of Christmas stickers.

Preparation: Trace Christmas Tree Birthday Card Pattern on green paper and cut one for each child. Fold and letter white paper as shown, one for each child.

Procedure: Child glues tree onto card and decorates card (and tree) with stars and stickers. Encourage child to "read" lettering with you.

Who will you give your Christmas card to? I'm glad for (name of person child chose to give card to), aren't you? How does (person) help you?

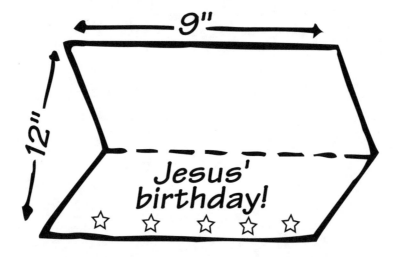

Christmas Crafts and Activities © 1998 by Gospel Light. Permission to photocopy granted.

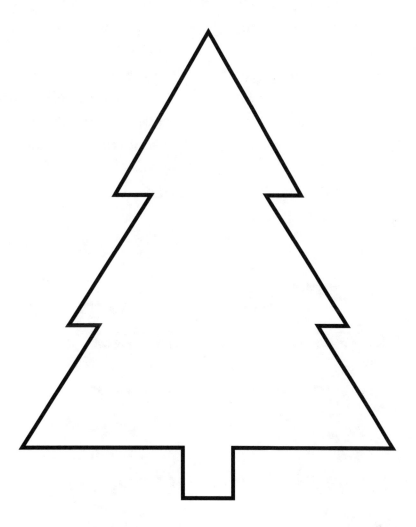

Circles of Love

Materials: Felt pen, construction paper, scissors, drawing compass or a circle pattern, ruler, 1/4-inch (.625-cm) ribbon in Christmas colors, hole punch, Christmas stickers.

Preparation: Using compass or circle pattern, outline and cut out three paper circles for each child. Cut ribbon into 6-inch (15-cm) lengths, three for each child. Add lettering to circles—both front and back—as shown. Punch holes in tops of circles.

Procedure: Give each child three circles and an assortment of stickers to decorate them with. Children thread ribbons through holes in circles, connecting circles and tying off ribbons as shown. Read the words on the circles with the children.

These words tell us why Christmas is so special. Our Bible says, "God loved us and sent His Son." God loves you and God loves me. That's why we celebrate Christmas!

Fold and Dangle Ornament

Materials: Red and green construction paper, pencil, measuring stick, scissors or paper cutter, ribbon, glue, hole punch.

Preparation: Cut paper into 1x18-inch (2.5x45-cm) strips—one red and one green for each child. Cut ribbon into 6-inch (15-cm) lengths—one for each child.

Procedure: Children glue ends of strips at right angles and then fold strips as shown, alternating red and green. Punch hole in end of strip and have children thread ribbon through hole. Tie for hanger.

Why do we like to decorate our homes and churches at Christmas? Christmas is Jesus' birthday. And we are glad! We can tell God, "Thank You for baby Jesus."

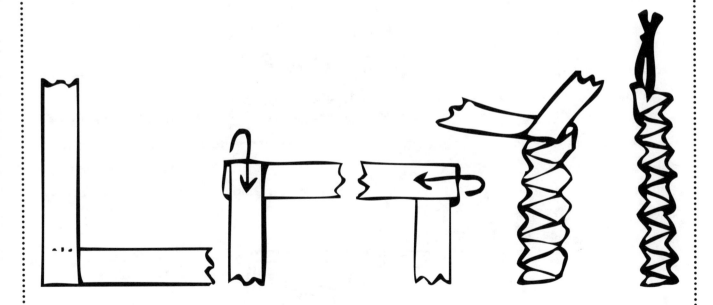

Christmas Wrap

Materials: Red and green tempera paint, water, shallow trays, newspaper, scissors, butcher paper, paper towels (or container of clear water), paint smocks (or old shirts), a variety of gadgets for printing (Christmas cookie cutters, Styrofoam packing material, string, small pieces of sponges or Styrofoam cut in different shapes such as stars and crosses, clothespins, tubes from paper towels, empty spools, corks); pencil, ruler; optional—white paint, colored paper.

Preparation: Mix tempera paint with just enough water to make it a fairly thick consistency. Place paint in shallow trays. Cover work area with newspaper.

Procedure: Put paint, paper towels (or container of clear water) and gadgets on newspaper. Give a square of butcher paper to each child. Children put on paint smocks and print designs by dipping one end of gadget into shallow pans of paint and then pressing gadget firmly onto the blank paper. (You may want to provide some paper for children to sample the design each gadget makes.) Encourage children to share gadgets as needed, being careful not to dip a gadget into another color of paint until it has been wiped off with paper towels (or dipped into container of clear water). If children wish to print designs in rows, use a pencil and ruler to mark guidelines on their papers. (Optional—Instead of or in addition to red and green paint and butcher paper, provide white paint and colored paper.)

We love to give and receive gifts at Christmastime. What kinds of gifts do you like to give to other people? You may use the pretty paper you made to wrap your Christmas gifts.

Feed the Birds

Materials: Wire, pinecones, cookie sheet, bird seed, table knives, peanut butter, lunch-sized paper bags.

Preparation: Wrap a piece of wire around the top of a pinecone so it may be hung (sketch a)—one for each child.

Procedure: Fill a cookie sheet with bird seed. Using a table knife, children spread peanut butter on the pinecones (sketch b). Children hold onto the wire and top portion of the pinecone and roll it in birdseed (sketch c). Children take pinecones home in paper bags and hang pinecones outside in a tree.

We always have good food to eat at Christmastime. What's your favorite Christmas food? God shows His care for us by giving us good things to eat. We can help care for the birds in cold weather by feeding them with these pinecones. It will be fun to watch the birds enjoy your gift. While you watch them eat, be sure to thank God for giving you good food, too!

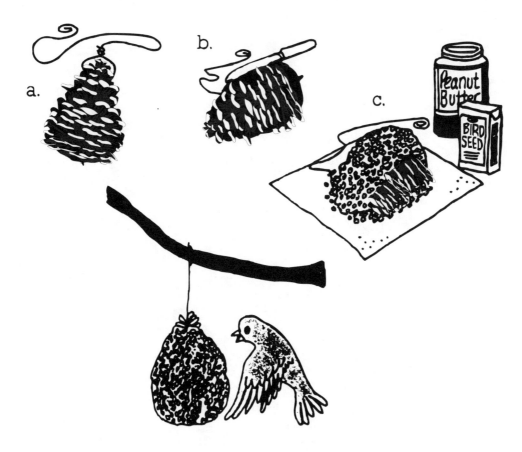

a.

b.

c.

Photo Frame

Materials: Pencil, lightweight cardboard, ruler, pencil, scissors, heavy poster board, craft knife, glue, felt pens, a variety of craft materials (ribbon, beads, buttons, fabric scraps, stickers, wrapping paper scraps and glitter glue); optional—instant camera and film.

Preparation: On lightweight cardboard, draw and cut out frame and stand patterns like those in sketches a and b. For each child, use patterns to draw and cut two frames (along outer edge only) and one stand from heavy poster board. Then use a craft knife to cut a window in one piece of each pair of frames. (Each child, then, will have three pieces: a solid back piece, a front piece with a window and a stand.)

Procedure: Children use a variety of craft materials to decorate the front piece of the photo frame. When the front of the frame is finished, the child turns it over and spreads glue along the edge of two sides and the bottom (sketch c). Then the child glues the front piece to the solid back piece. The child bends the end of the stand to form a tab as shown in sketch b and then glues the tab to the back of the picture frame (sketch d).

(Optional: Take instant snapshots of children to place in completed frames.)

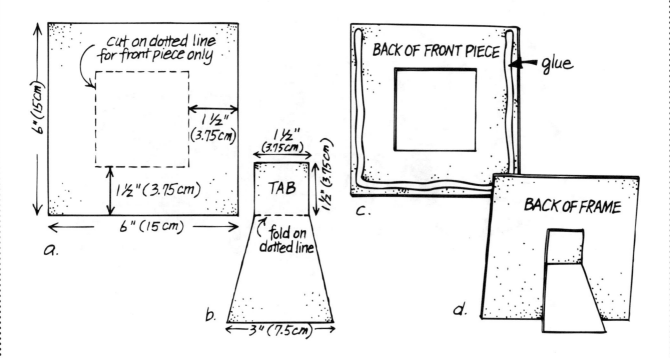

Nativity Scene

Materials: Bible, Nativity Scene Pattern (double-sided), photocopier, paper, scissors, tape, green, brown and tan construction paper, cotton balls, lunch-size paper bags.

Preparation: Photocopy one Nativity Scene Pattern for each child.

Procedure: Children cut apart and fold stable and figures from Nativity Scene Pattern. Demonstrate how to use tape to fasten stable together. Allow children time to set up their nativity scenes on sheets of construction paper. Children may add cotton balls for sheep and cut out trees, hills and buildings from construction paper. Tape these added features to the construction paper base. Each child uses his or her figures to act out the Christmas story. Ask questions to prompt children as they act out the story. Give each child a bag in which to take home the figures.

tape →

tape →

Crafts • **Lower Elementary**
Nativity Scene Pattern

Children cut on bold lines and
fold on broken lines.

Message Tissue Wreaths

Materials: Ruler, red and green tissue paper, scissors, 9-inch (22.5-cm) white paper plates, drawing compass, yarn, pencils with erasers, felt-tip pens, glue, hole punch; optional—pictures from magazines and used Christmas cards that show a scene from the story of Jesus' birth.

Preparation: Cut tissue paper into 1 1/2-inch (3.75-cm) squares. (Note: You'll need to cut more green squares than red.) On the front of each paper plate, draw a 4-inch (10-cm) circle in the center. Cut one 6-inch (15-cm) length of yarn for each child.

Procedure: Give each child a pencil, a felt-tip pen and one paper plate. In the center circle of their plates, children draw a picture or write a special message about the story of Jesus' birth. (Optional—glue magazine or greeting card pictures in center circle.) They cover a small area of the wreath (not the center circle) with glue. Then they wrap a green tissue square around the eraser end of pencil and press tissue onto wreath (see sketch a), repeating the procedure until wreath is almost covered. (Glue pieces of tissue close together to give wreath a full, puffy look.) They add a few squares of red tissue to represent berries. Punch a hole in paper plate at top of wreath and tie yarn through hole to make a hanger. (See sketch b.)

tissue square

glue

God Loves Us

a.

God Loves Us

b.

Place Mats

Materials: Newspapers, 11x14-inch (27.5x35-cm) sheets of lightweight poster board, a variety of craft items (used Christmas cards, butcher paper and marker or chalkboard and chalk, felt pens, scissors, glue, clear adhesive-backed plastic, seasonal pictures of a variety of subjects from magazines, holiday gift wrap, fabric scraps, rickrack, ribbon, glitter, stickers, pressed leaves or grasses, etc.), butcher paper and marker or chalkboard and chalk, felt pens, scissors, glue, clear adhesive-backed plastic.

Preparation: Cover work area with newspapers.

Procedure: Give each child a sheet of poster board. Show children the variety of craft materials. Have them think about making a place mat that will remind them to thank God when they sit down to eat. Help children think of short prayers or statements of praise they want to put on their place mats. Write suggestions on the butcher paper or chalkboard. Children write their reminders on the poster board and then decorate around them with the materials you brought.

When a child is finished decorating, help him or her to cover the poster board piece with clear adhesive-backed plastic. Peel off the backing on the plastic and spread the plastic on the table, sticky side up. Bend the poster board in the middle and carefully lower it onto the plastic. Work from the center out to the edges, rubbing firmly to remove air bubbles. Cover the front and the back of the poster board, pressing the plastic together around all four edges. The child then uses scissors to trim the excess plastic from around the edges of the place mat.

Bible Verse Doorknob Hanger

Materials: Bible, large sheet of butcher paper and marker or chalkboard and chalk, Doorknob Hanger Pattern, photocopier, card stock or lightweight cardboard, pencil, scissors, red and/or green poster board, materials to decorate hanger (ribbon, glitter, stickers, jingle bells, etc.), felt pens, glue.

Preparation: Letter a favorite Christmas verse on butcher paper or chalkboard. Copy the Doorknob Hanger Pattern onto card stock or lightweight cardboard. Trace around the pattern on poster board to make one hanger for each child. Cut out hangers. You may want to leave the edges for children to trim.

Procedure: Ask volunteers what they do to help them remember important things. Point out the verse you lettered on the paper as one you want to remember. Explain that you will make a special sign to remind you of that verse every time you enter or leave your room. Distribute hangers and materials for decorating. If you did not already do so, let children finish trimming around the edges of the hanger. Children letter verse on hangers and then use various materials to decorate them.

"Today in the town of David a Savior has been born to you." Luke 2:11

Crafts • **Lower Elementary**
Doorknob Hanger Pattern

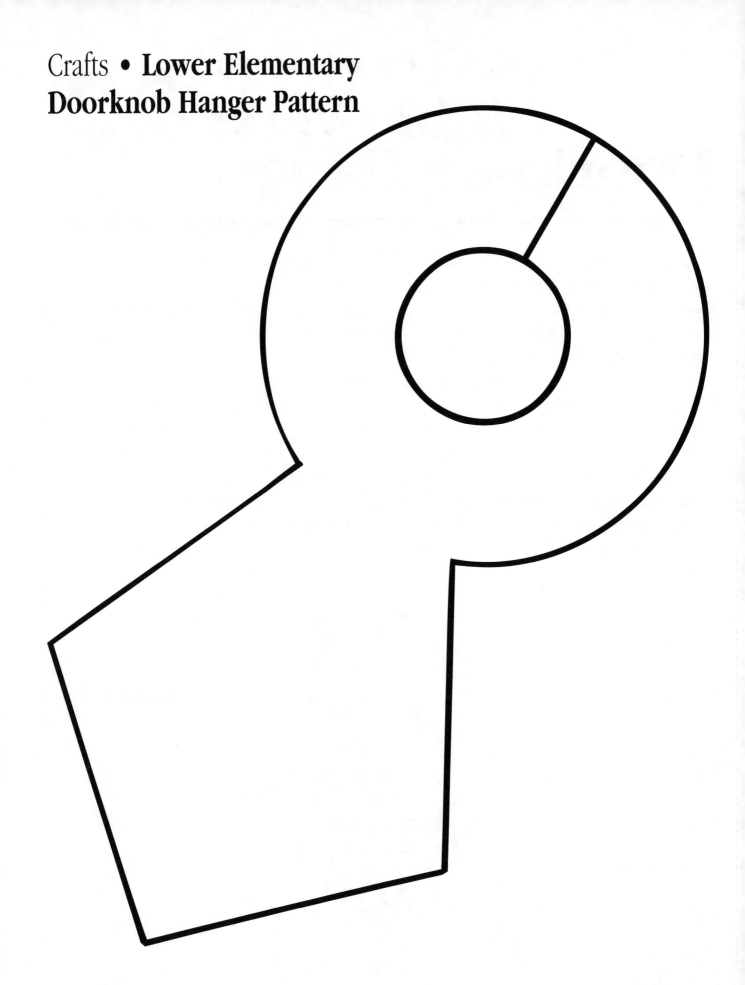

Christmas Crafts and Activities © 1998 by Gospel Light. Permission to photocopy granted.

Christmas Wind Sock

Materials: Measuring stick, red or green yarn or narrow ribbon, scissors, 9x12-inch (22.5x30-cm) sheets of red and green construction paper, glue, felt pens, a variety of decorating materials (Christmas stickers, Christmas rubber stamps and ink stamp pads, used Christmas cards, Christmas wrapping paper, glitter), clear adhesive-backed plastic, large stapler and staples, red and green crepe paper streamers, hole punch.

Preparation: Measure and cut yarn or ribbon into 18-inch (45-cm) lengths—one for each child. Then follow the directions to make a sample wind sock.

Procedure: Show the sample you prepared. Each child chooses a sheet of green or red paper. Children decorate only one side of their papers with drawings and/or materials.

Help each child cover the decorated paper with clear adhesive-backed plastic to protect the wind sock and make the wind sock sturdier. Peel off the backing on the plastic and spread the plastic on the table, sticky side up. Carefully lower the decorated paper onto the plastic. Work from the center out to the edges, rubbing firmly to remove air bubbles. Cover both sides of the paper, pressing the plastic together around all four edges. Children us scissors to trim the excess plastic from around the edges of the paper.

Make a tube of the decorated paper by overlapping the 9-inch (22.5-cm) sides and stapling. Each child cuts four or five crepe paper streamers of desired length and staples streamers along the inside bottom edge of the tube. Punch two holes along the top edge. Lace yarn or ribbon through holes and tie to make a hanger for the wind sock.

Stained-Glass Verse

Materials: Bible, large sheet of butcher paper and marker or chalkboard and chalk, white typing paper, ruler, scissors, colored poster board, felt-tip pens, newspapers, non-stick cooking spray, paper towels, glue.

Preparation: Letter 1 John 4:9 or another Christmas verse on butcher paper or chalkboard. Cut typing paper into 8 1/2-inch (21.5-cm) squares—one for each child. Cut poster board into 9 1/2-inch (23.75-cm) squares—two for each child. Cut a 6 1/2-inch (16.25-cm) square from the center of each poster board square to make a frame. (See sketch a.)

Procedure: Distribute paper squares and felt-tip pens. Instruct children to create a col-orful design on their papers. (See sketch b.) Children should outline the different parts of their designs in black. Next, children letter the verse you have chosen on their designs. (See sketch c.) Lettering should be at least 2 1/2 inches (6.25 cm) from each edge of the paper.

Place finished designs on newspapers. Spray lightly with a coat of nonstick cooking spray. Wipe off excess oil with paper towels. Allow to dry. The oil gives the colors a translucent quality. Put glue around edge of one frame. (See sketch d.) Children center design over glued frame. Carefully glue second frame on top of picture. Allow to dry.

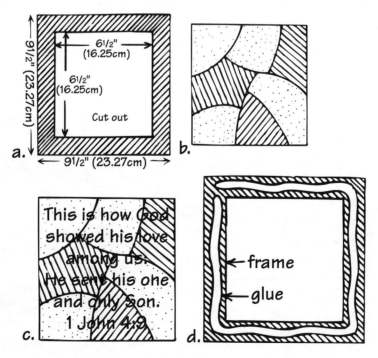

Gift Bag

Materials: Measuring stick, red or green yarn or narrow ribbon, scissors, lunch-size paper bags, a variety of decorating materials (glitter, rickrack, fancy braid, construction paper, Christmas stickers, Christmas rubber stamps and ink stamp pads, pictures cut from religious Christmas cards or wrapping paper), glue, transparent or masking tape, hole punch; optional—jingle bells, tissue paper.

Preparation: Cut yarn or ribbon into 18-inch (45-cm) lengths—two pieces for each child. Follow the directions to make a sample gift bag.

Procedure: Show the sample you prepared.

Give each child a paper bag. Children use materials provided to decorate their gift bags. Assist children as necessary with the following directions: Reinforce the top inside edges of bags with tape. Then punch two holes on front and back of each bag as shown in sketch. Lace yarn or ribbon through each pair of holes to make two handles on each bag. (Optional: Lace yarn or ribbon through jingle bells to attach bells to the handles. Line bags with tissue paper.)

Children may make gift cards to tape to their bags or they may write names of the gift

Shining Star

Materials: Dark blue construction paper, pencil, waxed paper, colored tissue paper, scissors, glue, felt pens, tape.

Preparation: Trace a star pattern on construction paper—one star for each child (see sketch b).

Procedure: Give each child a star pattern and a piece of waxed paper that is about the same size as the construction paper. Children cut or tear tissue paper into different shapes and glue the shapes to waxed paper with dots of glue. (See sketch a.) Then they cut out the construction paper star, keeping the frame. (See sketch b.) Children write a Christmas verse on the construction paper frames with felt pens and glue the frames to the tissue-covered waxed paper. (See sketch c.) Trim edges if needed. Tape star pictures in window to see light shining through the colored tissue.

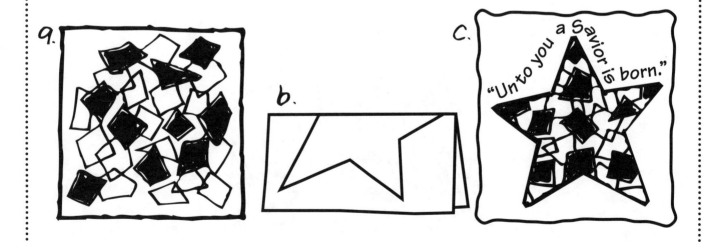

Stained-Glass Angel Poster

Materials: Various colors of construction paper (including black), scissors, glue, length of butcher paper, marker.

Preparation: Cut two large angel shapes from black construction paper. (See sketch a.)

Procedure: Children work together to cut small pieces of colored construction paper and glue them on the angels to give a stained-glass effect. Letter the words of Matthew 1:23b on the butcher paper and glue angels on either side of the verse. (See sketch b.) Display poster in your room or in a hallway.

a. Approx. 2 ft. (.6 m)

b. " They will call him, Immanuel— which means, 'God with us!'" Matthew 1:23

A Star Is Born!

Materials: Photocopier, paper, A Star Is Born! Pattern (double-sided), scissors, curling ribbon, measuring stick, tape, fine-tip felt pens.

Preparation: Photocopy one double-sided A Star Is Born! Pattern page for each child. Cut ribbon into 16-inch (40-cm) lengths—four for each child.

Procedure: Children cut out star pieces and slide them together to form star. (See sketch a.) Tape each child's star to secure it. (See sketch b.) Lead children to fill in answers (or draw a small stick figure picture) on the gift boxes about ways they can worship Jesus. Children cut out boxes. Give each child four ribbons. Children tie all four ribbons together at one end. Help children drape ribbons over star and tie together again under star. (See sketch c.) (Optional: Trim ends of ribbons to different lengths.) Then children tape a gift box to the end of each ribbon. Completed mobiles can be displayed on a bulletin board or hung from the ceiling.

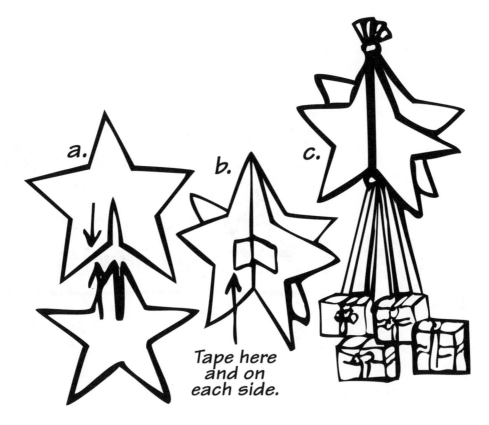

a.

b. Tape here and on each side.

c.

Crafts • Lower Elementary
A Star Is Born! Pattern

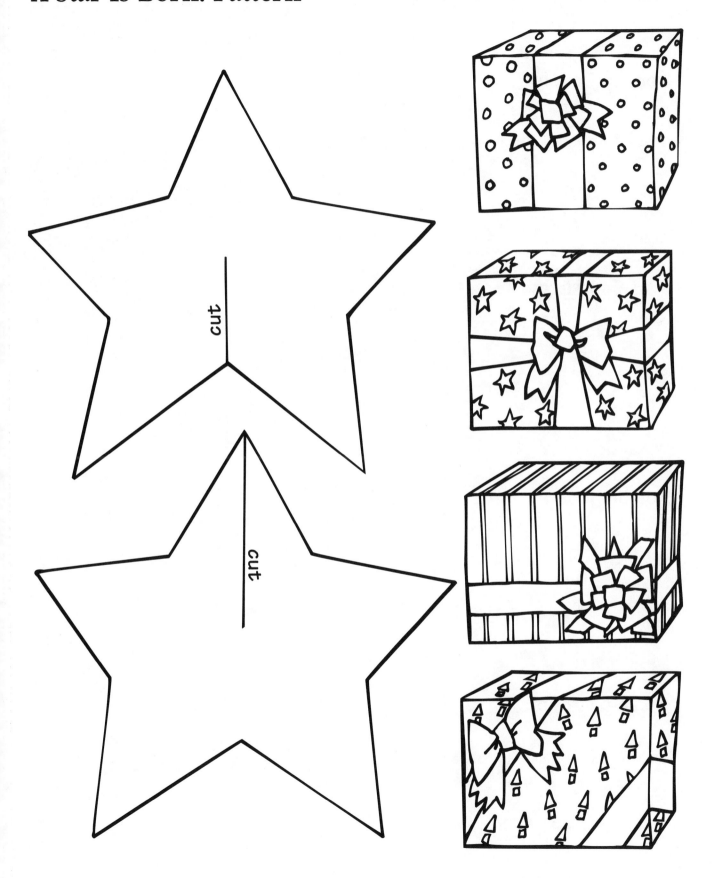

cut

cut

Crafts • **Lower Elementary**
A Star Is Born! Pattern

I worship Jesus by

I worship Jesus by

I worship Jesus by

I worship Jesus by

Manger Scene

Materials: Drawing compass, scissors, ruler, pink, light blue, brown and dark blue construction paper, fabric, yellow tissue paper, glue.

Preparation: Cut two pink construction paper circles, each 1 1/2 inches (3.75 cm) in diameter. Cut 2 1/2 x 4-inch (6.25x10-cm) rectangles out of light blue construction paper; then cut each rectangle diagonally in half to form triangles. Cut six narrow brown construction paper strips, two 6 1/2-inches (16.25-cm) long, two 4-inches (10 cm) long and two 2-inches (5 cm) long. Cut two head coverings from fabric. Make a sample manger scene for children to use as a guide.

Procedure: Give each child a sheet of dark blue construction paper, two pink circles, two light blue triangles, six brown strips (two of each length), two head coverings and a small piece of yellow tissue. Assist children in gluing items on construction paper to assemble manger scene.

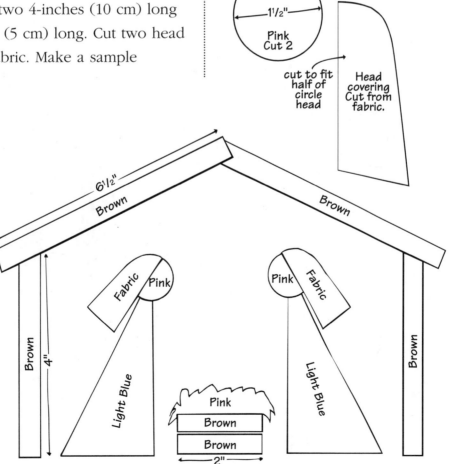

Paper Plate Angel

Materials: Large flexible paper plates, pencil, scissors, ruler, yarn, crayons or felt-tip pens, small gold or white doily, glue, stars, foil wrapping paper, stapler and staples, tape, hole punch, glitter.

Preparation: For each child, cut angel from paper plate as shown. Cut yarn into 12-inch (30-cm) lengths.

Procedure: Child draws face on angel. Help child staple robe in front, glue doily behind head for halo and stick stars or glue foil onto robe. Guide child in folding wings down and stapling or taping to back of robe. Punch hole in top of head. Thread yarn through the hole and tie. Spread glue on underside of skirt, sprinkle glitter and shake off excess. Hang angel and let it fly in the breeze!

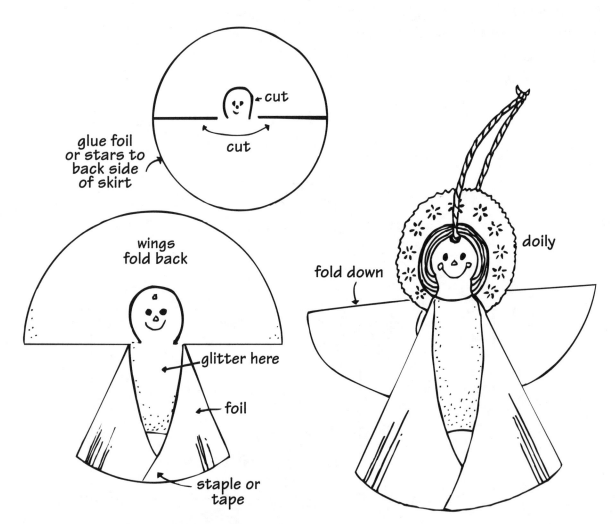

Heavenly Hosts

Materials: Heavenly Hosts Angel Pattern, cardboard or construction paper, pencils, scissors, long sheets of paper (newsprint, Christmas wrapping paper or tissue paper); optional—Bible, markers.

Preparation: Trace and cut out one Heavenly Hosts Angel Pattern from cardboard or construction paper for every 3 to 4 children.

Procedure: Child folds a large sheet of paper and then traces and cuts a row of three or six angels. (Optional: Help child letter a short Christmas verse across the row of angels.) **Hang your heavenly hosts around your room and let them help fill your day with Christmas praises!**

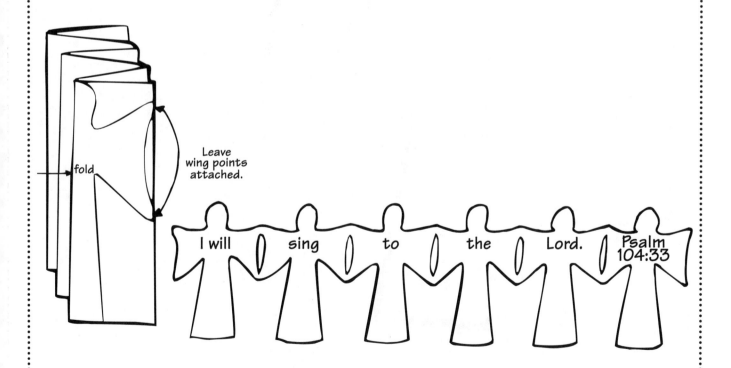

fold

Leave wing points attached.

I will sing to the Lord. Psalm 104:33

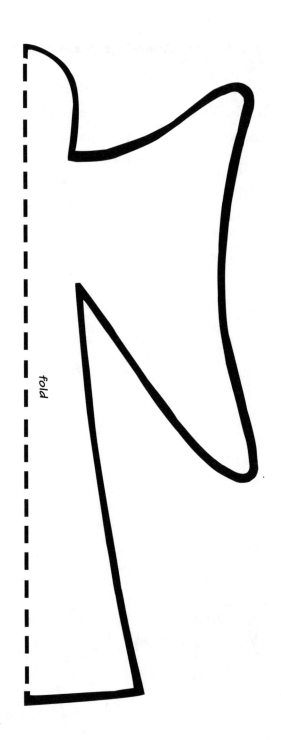

fold

Baker's Clay Ornaments

Materials: Flour, salt, water, large bowl, wooden spoon, resealable plastic bag, waxed paper, cookie cutters of various shapes, large buttons, pencil, oven, cookie sheets, clear varnish or plastic spray, acrylic paints, brushes, string or yarn.

Preparation: Make baker's clay by combining 4 cups flour, 1 cup salt and 1 1/2 cups water in a large bowl. Stir mixture until all dry ingredients are moistened. (This recipe will make about 12 ornaments.) Knead dough on floured surface for five minutes. Place dough in plastic bag and use as needed.

Procedure: Give each child a small ball of dough and a sheet of waxed paper on which to work. Children press dough to 1-inch

(2.5 cm) thickness. They may leave it in that shape or cut out a shape with a cookie cutter. Children then decorate their ornaments by making impressions with buttons or by layering dough "ropes" of various thicknesses around edges of the ornaments (use water to make dough stick to itself). With a pencil, make a small hole through top of ornament.

Bake ornaments on cookie sheet at 350 degrees for 30-45 minutes. Test for doneness by pressing down with back of spoon. Clay is done when the spoon does not make an indentation. Allow to cool for 10 minutes and then spray with clear varnish or plastic. Decorate with paint as desired. Thread string or yarn through hole for hanging.

Gift Tags and Cards

Materials: Light-colored construction paper, ruler, pencil, scissors, hole punch, burlap, foil wrapping paper, glue, used Christmas cards, string or yarn.

Preparation: Cut construction paper into 2x3-inch (5x7.5-cm) rectangles for gift tags and into 12x8 1/2-inch (30x21.5-cm) rectangles for note cards. Punch holes near left edge of tags. Provide at least one gift tag and note card for each child.

Procedure: Distribute the rectangles you prepared. Have children fold larger rectangles in half to make note cards (see sketch a). Children cut burlap or foil wrapping paper in shapes smaller than tags or cards and then fringe the edges of the burlap by pulling out a few threads on all four sides. Children glue burlap or foil shapes to fronts of tags and notes (see sketch b). Children then cut out a small picture from used Christmas cards and glue the picture to burlap or foil (see sketch c). Children cut short length of string or yarn to make a tie for each gift tag.

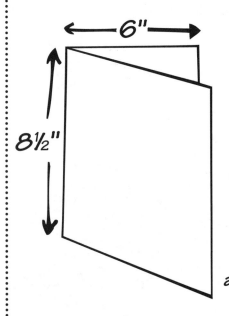

a.

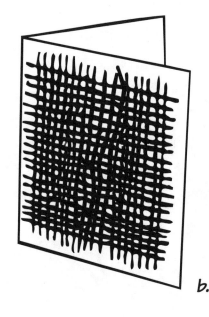

b.

c.

Stitched Christmas Cards

Materials: Construction paper, rulers, pencils, scissors, butcher paper and marker, tape, lightweight card-size poster board, darning needles, yarn of various colors, glue, sequins.

Preparation: Cut sheets of construction paper so that they are about 1/4 inch (.625 cm) smaller than poster-board cards. Tape butcher paper in a visible place. Make a sample card following the directions given below.

Procedure: Brainstorm with children a list of words or symbols associated with Christmas and record them on butcher paper. On butcher paper, show the children how the words or items on the list can be drawn or written using only straight lines. Show the sample card you made. Give each child a poster-board card. Children use pencils and rulers to draw the designs of their choice on their cards. Each child then uses a darning needle to punch holes at the end points of all lines. Cut a length of yarn for each child and help thread needles with it. Starting from back of card, child stitches through holes, leaving about 6 inches (15 cm) of yarn dangling at the back. When stitching is completed, child securely ties together dangling ends. Glue construction paper to back of card to cover stitching and glue sequins to front of card for additional decoration.

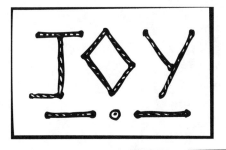

Tissue Paper Ball Ornaments

Materials: Lightweight poster board, drawing compass, pencil, scissors, hole punch, ruler, tissue paper in bright colors, yarn or ribbon, newspapers, glue.

Preparation: Draw 3-inch (7.5-cm) circles on poster board and cut out at least one circle for each child. Punch a hole near the top of each circle. Cut tissue paper into 1/2-inch (1.25-cm) squares. Cut yarn or ribbon into 6-inch (15-cm) lengths, one for each ornament. Cover work area with newspapers.

Procedure: Children choose squares of tissue paper and crumple them into balls. Then they spread glue on a section of their poster-board circles and stick tissue paper balls on circles. Children continue applying glue and tissue balls section by section until all but the punched hole is covered. Thread a piece of yarn or ribbon through the hole and tie it to make a hanger.

Paper Stars

Materials: Tissue paper in various colors, pencil, ruler, scissors, hole punch, string or yarn.

Preparation: Cut tissue paper into 8-inch (20-cm) squares. Make a sample star following illustrated directions.

Procedure: Show sample star you have made. Children make their own stars by following your example as you demonstrate the folds and the scissors cut. Children make as many stars as time permits. Children use hole punch to make hole at the top of one of the star's points and loop a length of string or yarn through it to make a hanger.

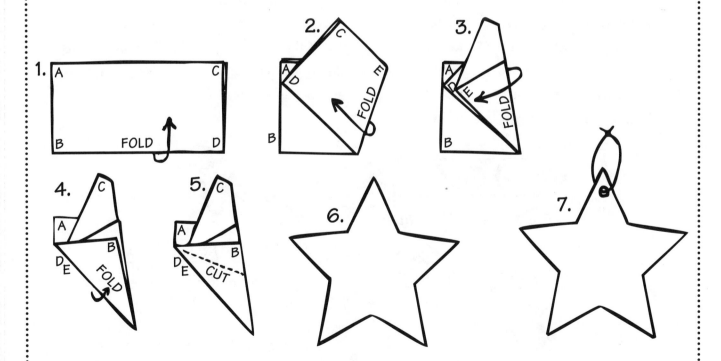

Felt Napkin Holder

Materials: Napkin Holder Pattern, photocopier, paper, scissors, pencil, lightweight cardboard, ruler, pieces of green felt, butcher paper and marker or chalkboard and chalk, fine-line dark felt pens, red sequins, red yarn, craft glue; optional—Christmas napkins.

Preparation: Photocopy the Napkin Holder Pattern and cut out. Make several patterns from lightweight cardboard for children to use. Cut green felt into 3x11-inch (7.5x27.5-cm) rectangles—at least two for each child.

Procedure: Brainstorm with children words that communicate the message of Christmas ("joy," "peace," "Jesus," "love," etc.) and record them on the butcher paper or chalkboard. Distribute two felt pieces to each child. (If you have enough felt, allow children to make napkin holders for all of their family members.) Children use felt pens to trace around the Napkin Holder Pattern on both felt pieces and then cut them out. (Don't forget to cut the slits as shown.) Use sequins and yarn to decorate the napkin holders. Yarn may be glued on to spell out one of the words from the list (see sketch a). Let glue dry thoroughly.

Demonstrate how to form the napkin holders by inserting and pulling the end labeled "Slit 1" through the opening labeled "Slit 2." (See sketches b and c.) You will need to roll the end of the felt slightly to slip it through the opening. (Optional: Insert Christmas napkins in the finished napkin holders as shown in sketch d.)

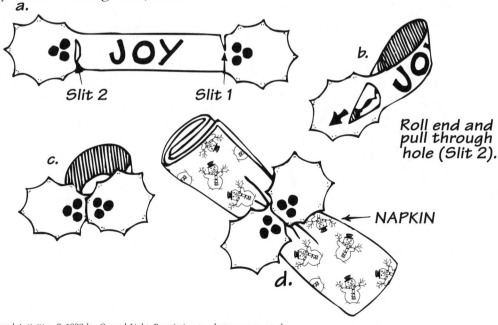

a.

JOY

Slit 2   Slit 1

b.

JOY

Roll end and pull through hole (Slit 2).

c.

NAPKIN

d.

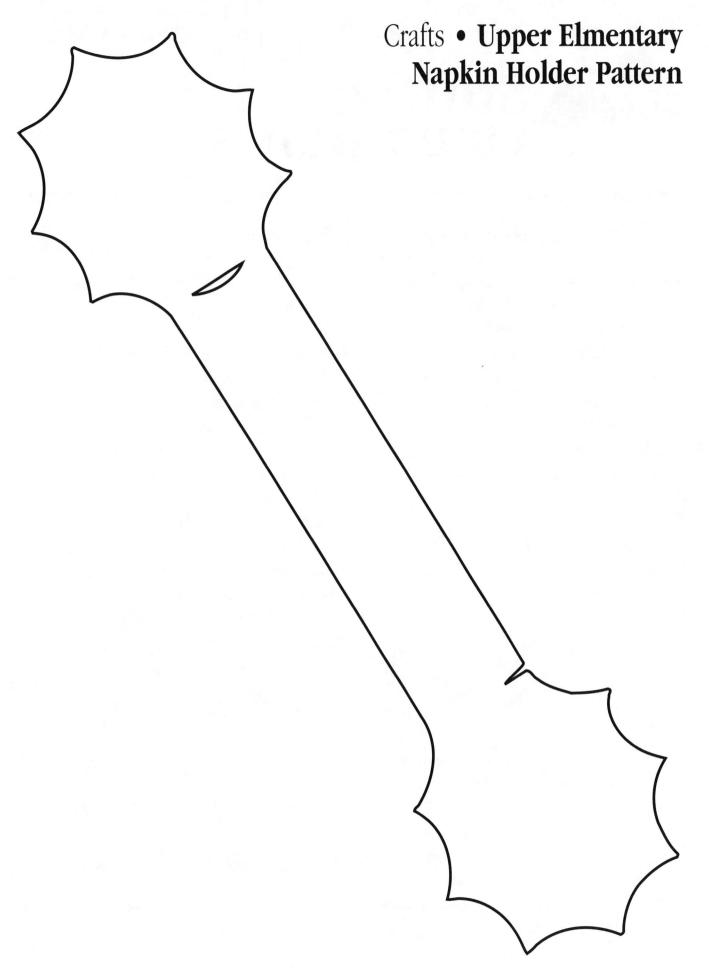

Stuffed Ornaments

Materials: Heavy paper or cardboard, pencils, scissors, large brown paper bags, hole punch, glue, glitter, fabric scraps, felt pens, yarn, tape, newspapers; optional—Christmas coloring books, used Christmas cards.

Preparation: Using heavy paper or cardboard, draw and cut out patterns of simple Christmas shapes (i.e., bells, trees, stars). (Optional: Patterns may be traced from sources such as Christmas coloring books.) Cut paper bags into pieces slightly larger than the patterns (two pieces per child).

Procedure: Distribute two paper bag pieces to each child.

a.

Children choose a pattern for their ornaments, trace it on both of their bag pieces and cut them out. (Each child should have two of the same shape.) Holding pieces together, children punch holes around the edges with hole punch (see sketch a). Children then decorate the fronts and backs of their ornaments with glitter, fabric scraps and/or felt pen designs. (Optional—Children may choose to cut a shape around the art on a Christmas card to be their ornament. They would need to cut a piece of paper bag in the same shape to be the back side of the ornament; holes can then be punched around edges of both pieces.)

Cut long lengths of yarn and have children wrap one end of yarn with tape to serve as a "needle." Children lace ornament pieces together around the edges, leaving an opening along one side through which to stuff crumpled newspaper scraps. When the ornament is stuffed, the lacing can be finished (see sketch b). Be sure to securely tie together yarn ends where they meet. Tie a loop of yarn at the top of the ornament for hanging. While children work, ask questions to discuss what the various shapes and symbols mean in relationship to Jesus' birth.

b.

Bible Verse Wreath

Materials: Bibles, sheets of red and green construction paper or felt, fine-line felt pens, scissors, stapler and staples, white paper, red or green yarn or narrow ribbon, glue, facial tissue or cotton balls.

Preparation: Make at least one sample wreath as described in directions. If you have time, make both a heart-shaped wreath and a round wreath.

Procedure: Show sample wreath(s). Children choose to make heart-shaped or round wreaths. (Demonstrate how to make a heart-shaped wreath by folding two sheets of paper or felt in half, drawing shape and cutting as shown in sketch a.) Each child cuts two identical pieces to make front and back of wreath. Child then staples pieces together along inner and outer edges of wreath, leaving some areas open along the inside edge for stuffing. Children may letter the words of a Bible verse or Christmas song along the outside edge of the wreath as shown in sketch c. They may also cut a small heart from white paper, letter the words on it and attach the heart with yarn or ribbon as shown in sketch b. Children then decorate wreaths with felt pens, paper and yarn or ribbon. Stuff wreaths with torn tissue or cotton balls to make them puffy; then finish stapling the inside edges. Attach a yarn hanger at top of each wreath.

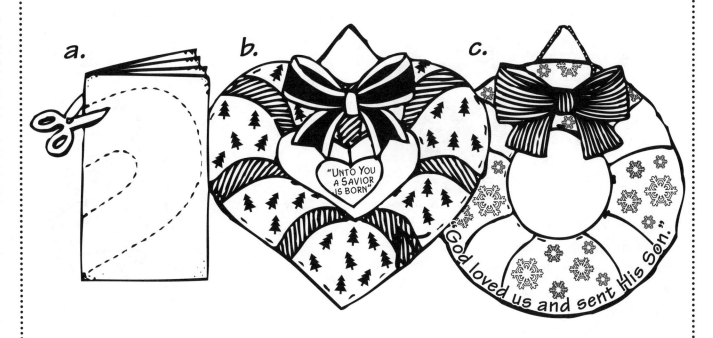

A Gift of Light

Materials: Bibles, pencil, ruler, white construction paper, scissors, hole punch, felt pens, ribbon, materials for the gift you choose to make.

Preparation: Make gift tags by cutting 2x3-inch (5x7.5-cm) rectangles from paper and punching a hole in one corner of each rectangle. Make one of the candles as a sample.

Procedure: Show sample candle. Talk about Jesus as "the light of the world." Children choose to make one of the following candles as a gift. Encourage children to name people to whom they will give their gifts and tell what they would like those recipients to know about Jesus.

Luminaries

Assist children in following these instructions: Cut a heavy piece of paper to fit around a wide-mouthed, clear glass jar, forming a cylinder as tall as the jar. Draw a design on the paper and then cut away sections of the paper to let light through. When cuts are complete, glue a sheet of tissue paper or cellophane to the back of the heavy paper. Trim excess paper. Wrap the paper around the jar and tape or glue edges together (see sketch a). Pour 1 inch (2.5 cm) of sand into the jar. Stand a votive candle upright in the sand.

a.

Stained-Glass Jar

Pour some glue into a container and dilute with water. Stir until the solution is the consistency of milk. Help children as necessary in following these instructions: Tear or cut various colors of tissue paper into small pieces. Hold a wide-mouthed, clear glass jar upside down on two extended fingers (see sketch

b.

b). Brush glue solution onto a small section of the outside of the jar and cover the glued area with tissue paper pieces. Continue the process section by section until all but the mouth and the bottom of the jar are covered with overlapping pieces of tissue paper. Then lightly brush a layer of glue solution over the tissue pieces to smooth the edges and set the design. Let dry. Add sand and candle as directed for luminaries (see sketch c).

Jesus is the Light.

c.

Christmas Candle

Give a small candle to each child. Children use brushes to paint white glue around outside of candle. Children attach a variety of small flat decorations (glitter, small evergreen needles, tiny pinecones, stickers, holiday confetti, etc.) to the candle (see sketch d). A final coat of glue over the decorations insures stability.

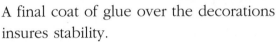

d.

Gift Tags

On the construction paper tags, have children write a message that will be a reminder that Jesus is the light of the world. Refer children to 1 John 1:5, John 8:12 or Isaiah 60:19 in their Bibles. Children may choose to simply letter "Jesus is the light" on their tags. Children then cut a length of ribbon, thread it through the hole in the tag and tie it around the mouth of the jar (see sketch c) or the middle of the candle.

Peace Christmas Cards

Materials: Bibles, butcher paper and marker or chalkboard and chalk, construction paper, scissors, glue, a variety of decorating materials, felt pens, used Christmas cards, Christmas wrapping paper, ribbon, glitter glue.

Procedure: With children, read aloud Isaiah 9:6. Explain that children will be making Christmas cards to illustrate that Jesus is the Prince of Peace. Brainstorm words, phrases and symbols for peace with children and list them on the butcher paper or chalkboard.

Children fold sheets of construction paper in half to make cards. Then they decorate the fronts of the cards with a variety of materials and/or drawings to illustrate the idea of peace. They may also glue peaceful scenes and/or appropriate words cut from used Christmas cards or Christmas wrapping paper to cards. Pieces of ribbon and glitter glue may be used for added decoration. As children work, talk about the ways in which following Jesus can bring peace in our relationships.

Story Quilt

Materials: Coloring book with pictures of the life of Jesus, fabric paints, 10x10-inch (25x25-cm) fabric squares, needles, thread, sewing machine, quilt stuffing, quilt backing, yarn.

Procedure: Using the coloring book pages as patterns, children draw or trace pictures that tell the story of Jesus onto separate quilt squares with fabric paint. Sew squares together, using fabric borders in between. Complete quilt with stuffing and backing. Use yarn ties along seams and at corners to hold quilt together. Give the quilt as a gift to a special member of the church or raffle it as a fund-raiser.

Berry Basket Snowflakes

Materials: Newspapers, scissors, clean berry baskets, hot-glue gun, white or silver spray paint, glitter, yarn.

Preparation: Cover work area with newspapers.

Procedure: Children make snowflakes by cutting shapes from the bottoms of baskets and gluing them together with a hot-glue gun. (You may want to handle the glue gun.) Children then spray one side of plastic with white or silver spray paint and sprinkle glitter on wet paint. Let paint dry completely before other side is similarly decorated. Children tie loops of yarn to tops of "snowflakes" to hang.

Christmas String Angel

Materials: Photocopier, paper, glue, water, shallow containers, newspaper, heavy string, small plastic soda bottles, glitter, waxed paper, round gold Christmas ornaments, gold chenille wire.

Preparation: Photocopy the sketches so each child will more easily be able to follow the directions. Dilute glue with water and pour into containers. Cover work area with newspaper.

Day One Procedure: Assist children in following these instructions: Dip heavy string in diluted glue and then evenly wind the string around a plastic soda bottle to form angel body (see sketch a). Sprinkle glitter over body. Lay other pieces of glue-soaked string on waxed paper in a double wing shape and fill in outline with coiled designs (see sketch b). Sprinkle glitter over wings. Allow to dry overnight.

Day Two Procedure: Glue wings to back of angel. Glue gold ornament to top of body for a head. Shape chenille wire into a halo and glue on angel's head. (See sketch c.)

a.

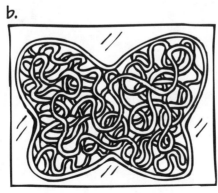

b.

c.

Make-Your-Own Gift Box

Materials: Make-Your-Own Gift Box Pattern, photocopier, paper, scissors, pencils, card stock, glue, tape.

Preparation: Photocopy one Gift Box Pattern for each child. Make a sample box according to directions below.

Procedure: Give each child a copy of the pattern. Instruct children in the following steps: Cut out the pattern. Trace the outline of the pattern onto card stock, marking fold lines, and cut out. Glue the paper pattern and the card-stock copy together so that the words on the paper pattern face out. Fold on dotted lines. Lay a piece of tape on the sides of square #1. Join #2 and #4 squares to #1, pressing onto tape. Bring up #3 square and tape from inside as for #1. Tuck flap in so bow is on top!

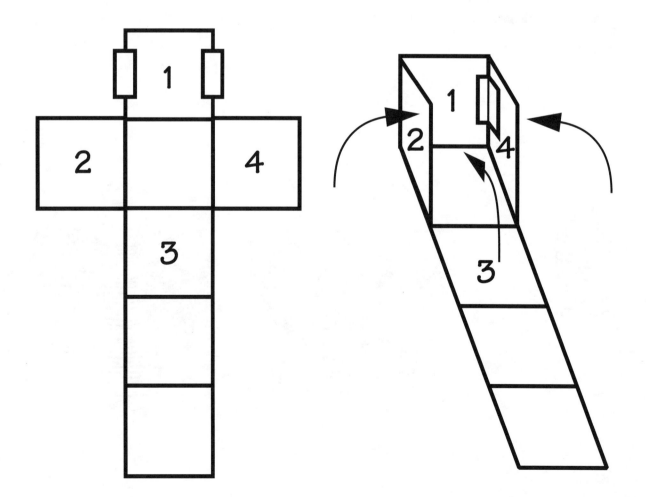

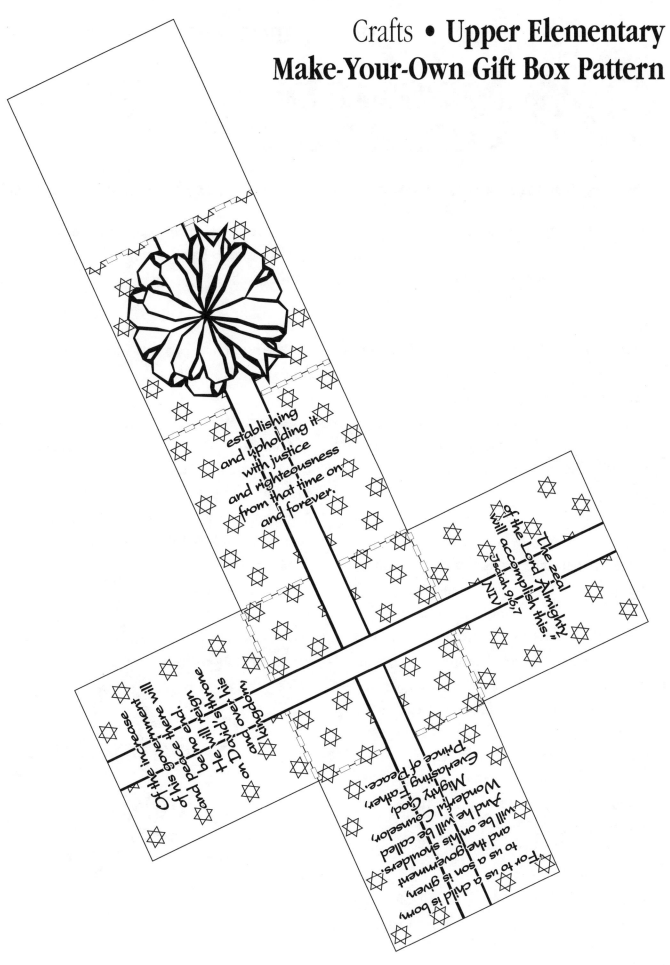

establishing
and upholding it
with justice
and righteousness
from that time on
and forever.

"The zeal
of the Lord Almighty
will accomplish this."
Isaiah 9:6,7
(NIV)

Of the increase
of his government
and peace end.
will be no reign
He will's throne
on David over his
and kingdom"

For to us a child is born,
to us a son is given,
and the government
will be on his shoulders,
And he will be called
Wonderful Counselor,
Mighty God,
Everlasting Father,
Prince of Peace.

Messiah Ornaments

Materials: Bibles, newspapers, clay/dough of your choice, waxed paper, sponges, water in small container, rolling pins, Christmas cookie cutters, pencils, string or narrow ribbon, scissors.

Preparation: Cover work area with newspapers. Make a sample ornament.

Procedure: Children find Isaiah 9:6 in their Bibles and read the names of Jesus found there. Each child chooses one of the names to put on his or her ornament. Show the sample ornament you made.

Give each child a 3-inch (7.5-cm) ball of clay. Children lightly moisten two pieces of waxed paper with sponge dipped in water and place slightly flattened ball of clay between them. Children roll out clay to a 3/8-inch (.94-cm) thickness and remove top piece of waxed paper. Children use cookie cutters to cut out shapes of their choice and then poke a hole near the top of each with a pencil. Children use pencils to carve in their ornaments the name of Jesus that they have selected. When shape is dry, thread a length of string or ribbon through the hole and tie to make a hanger.

Clay/Dough Ideas

1. Air-drying clay (available from craft or art supply stores): Follow package instructions for drying times.

2. Polymer clay (available from craft or art supply stores): Bake ornaments as instructed on the package.

3. Flour/salt dough: Mix 1 1/2 cups flour, 1 cup cornstarch, 1 cup salt and 1 cup warm water to make a pliable dough that will air dry.

4. Applesauce dough: Mix 1 cup applesauce, 1 1/2 cups cinnamon and 1/3 cup non-toxic white glue together to form a ball. Refrigerate for at least 30 minutes (or overnight). Roll out dough to a 1/4 inch (.625 cm) thickness. Ornaments should be allowed to dry for about two days before inserting strings or ribbons into holes.

Angel Bookmark

Materials: Bibles, Angel Bookmark Pattern, photocopier, paper, pencil, scissors, 7x11-inch (17.5x27.5-cm) white poster board, various colors of grosgrain ribbon, ruler, felt pens and crayons, stapler and staples, glue.

Preparation: Photocopy Angel Bookmark Pattern and transfer onto poster board. Cut one poster-board bookmark per child. For streamers, cut ribbon in 6-inch (15-cm) lengths. For waistband, cut ribbon into 3-inch (7.5-cm) lengths.

Procedure: Give children angel bookmarks and direct them to use pens and crayons to draw facial features and color hair. Children staple ribbon streamers to waist of angel (see sketch a). Then children glue waistband around top edge of ribbon to hide raw edges (see sketch b) and glue ends of waistband to back of bookmark (see sketch c).

Help children find references in their Bibles for the Christmas story (Luke 1:26-38, Matthew 1:20-24, Luke 2:8-14). Have children write a Bible verse on back of bookmark (e.g., "Glory to God in the highest"). Show children how to use the angel bookmark by placing the arms of the angel across the page they want to mark and the body of the angel behind it. Streamers can be used to mark other pages.

Games

Game Tips

Children of all ages need lots of time and space to move around. Many children learn best while moving.  Also, when kids can let off steam through physical activity, they are better prepared mentally and emotionally for more reflective activities. This selection of active games for elementary children will accomplish solid learning goals while helping to release any pent-up energy.

Games for elementary children should first of all be fun, but they can also help reinforce truths about Christmas that you want your children to learn. To make each game fun and profitable, observe the following:

• Explain the rules or process clearly and simply.

• Offer a "practice round," especially if the game is new. Children will learn the rules best by actually playing the game.

• Choose games appropriate to the skill levels of the children involved. If you know that some children are not able to read or write as well as others, avoid playing games which depend solely on that skill for success.

• Vary the process by which teams are formed. Allow children to group themselves into teams.  Play the game one time; then announce that the person on each team who is wearing the most (red) should rotate to another team. Play the game again. Vary the method of rotation so that children play with several different children each time.

Follow the Star

Materials: Bible, butcher paper, felt pen, tape, index cards, paper bag, construction paper, scissors, star-shaped cookies; optional—a nativity display.

Preparation: Write the words from Psalm 95:6 on butcher paper and tape paper to wall. Then write the verse on index cards, grouping words/phrases to fit size of group (one card per child). Letter a different manner of movement on each index card ("tiptoe," "walk backwards," "hop," "march," etc.). Put cards in paper bag. Cut out several stars from construction paper and tape them to the floor in a wandering path.

Procedure: Discuss with children how and why the wise men traveled to find Jesus when He was born. Read Psalm 95:6 from the paper you prepared and point out that the wise men bowed and worshiped Jesus when they gave Him their gifts. Children draw a card from the bag and follow the path of stars across the floor, moving according to the directions on the index card. (Enjoy the silly way of moving; this will help the children enjoy the game.)

At the end of the star path, children bow and say, "Come let us worship and bow down." Then they kneel and say, "Let us kneel before the Lord our Maker." Let children draw cards and follow the stars several times. On the last time down the path, serve children star-shaped cookies. (Optional: Have the star path lead to a nativity display.)

Who Am I?

Materials: Paper, felt pen.

Procedure: Lead children to name characters in the Christmas story (Jesus, Mary, Joseph, angel, shepherds, Herod, wise men). Write names on paper, asking enough questions about the characters to briefly review the Christmas story. Then lead children to play a guessing game. While one volunteer moves away from the group, help the other children secretly choose one of the Bible story characters from the list. When the volunteer returns to the group, he or she asks yes or no questions to determine the chosen character. If the answer to the child's question is yes, group stands up. If the answer to the child's question is no, group remains seated. After all characters have been guessed, discuss what the different characters knew about Jesus.

Christmas Cube Roll

Materials: Square box, tape, red or green wrapping paper, six different pictures of Christmas scenes from cards or gift wrap, glue.

Preparation: Tape lid on box. Cover box with red or green wrapping paper. Cut six different Christmas scenes from cards or gift wrap to fit box. Glue one picture to each side of box.

Procedure: Children take turns rolling the cube and explaining how the picture they roll (the picture that is faceup when cube stops moving) relates to Christmas. When appropriate, ask questions to help children discuss the pictures. **Who are the people in this picture? What is happening in the picture? What are the people in this picture (discovering, showing that they know) about Jesus? How does this picture show us that Jesus' birth was special?**

Christmas Story Circle

Materials: Christmas carol cassette/CD and player, Christmas ornament, individually wrapped candy.

Procedure: Children sit in a circle around the wrapped candy. Play a Christmas carol cassette/CD. Children play a game similar to Hot Potato, passing an ornament around the circle. When the music stops, the child holding the object tells a part of the Christmas story. When the music starts, the ornament is passed again. When the music stops, the child with the ornament tells another part of the Christmas story. Continue playing until the entire story has been told. Unwrap and eat the candy as you discuss favorite parts of the Christmas story.

Christmas Go Fish

Materials: Large sheet of paper, marker, index cards (six for each child), pencils, felt-tip pens, Christmas stickers.

Preparation: Draw lines to divide the large sheet of paper into six sections. Write a word from the Christmas story in each section ("Jesus," "angel," "manger," "shepherd," "Mary," "Joseph").

Procedure: Give each child six index cards. Children copy the six words—one word on each card—and decorate cards with felt-tip pens and Christmas stickers. Collect all cards and shuffle them together.

Lead children in playing a game similar to Go Fish. Place all cards facedown in a pile. Each child takes a turn to choose four cards. Children look at their cards to see what they need in order to make a set of six different cards. First player asks any other player for a card he or she needs. If child asked has the card, he or she must give the card to the player, ending the first player's turn. If child asked does not have the card, the first player chooses a card from the pile. Play continues until one child has collected all six words and places the cards faceup on table or floor. Player who won tells something he or she knows about the Christmas story using two of the six words. Repeat game as time permits.

Celebration Bowl

Materials: Masking tape, soft ball (sponge or Nerf ball), Christmas carols cassette/CD and player.

Preparation: Make a masking-tape line on the floor on one side of an open area in the room.

Procedure: Have one volunteer stand with ball behind masking-tape line. Another child volunteers to retrieve the ball. In the open area opposite the line, arrange remaining children in a triangle as human "bowling pins." Play a Christmas carol while children who are "bowling pins" march in time with the music. Bowler rolls ball on floor, trying to hit the foot of a "bowling pin" while it is on the floor. When a "bowling pin" is hit, he or she tells a way people today celebrate the birth of Jesus. Volunteer retrieves ball. Bowler has three tries to hit a "bowling pin." If no "bowling pin" is hit after three attempts, bowler calls out, "Freeze!" All "bowling pins" must stop marching and bowler gets one more turn to roll ball.

Continue game as time permits, with new bowlers for each round. Vary the game by asking hit "bowling pins" to tell a favorite part of the Christmas story or tell one reason they are thankful Jesus was born.

Who Said It?

Materials: Index cards, marker, six chairs, paper bag.

Preparation: Write each of the following instructions on separate index cards: "hop," "jump," "skip," "crawl," "walk backwards," "crab walk." Place chairs as shown.

Procedure: Brainstorm with children different statements made by people in the in the Christmas story. It may help to ask questions. **What did the angel say to Mary? What did Herod say to the wise men?**

Write one quote on the back of each index card you prepared. Place cards in the paper bag. Place the paper bag on the first chair. Children line up behind that chair. The first child picks a card from the bag, reads the quote and tells who said it. Child then does action written on reverse side of card to weave between the chairs and back to the line. Repeat game, asking each player to tell something they know about Jesus.

Guess the Gift!

Materials: Several small items (a bag of marbles, book, ball, etc.), wrapping paper, tape, ribbon, small slips of paper or Post-it Notes, pencils.

Preparation: Wrap each gift so as to conceal its shape, size and identity. Place wrapped gifts around the room.

Procedure: Allow children to handle each gift and try to guess what it is. Children write their guesses on slips of paper or Post-it Notes and place them near the gifts. Ask a volunteer to read guesses aloud. Then have other volunteers unwrap the gifts.

(Challenge: If you have room, divide children into groups, one group for each item. Each group secretly wraps the item to disguise it. Groups guess what the items might be.) Talk about how surprising it was to discover what the gifts really were. Discuss with children how God surprised people at the very first Christmas with the most wonderful gift of all.

Christmas Quiz

Materials: Bibles, used Christmas cards showing pictures from the story of Jesus' birth, scissors, glue, paper, pencils.

Preparation: Make a sample quiz paper by gluing a picture from a used Christmas card at the top of a piece of paper and writing five questions about the picture below it (see suggested questions below).

Procedure: Show children the quiz paper you prepared. Let volunteers take turns reading and answering the questions. Then ask each child to choose a picture and make a similar quiz paper. Refer children to these Bible passages for ideas: Mary and Joseph—Matthew 1:18-24, Luke 1:26-38; Jesus' birth—Luke 2:1-7; shepherds—Luke 2:8-20; wise men—Matthew 2:1-12; escape to Egypt—Matthew 2:13-18. If necessary, suggest questions, such as, "What are the names of the people in this picture?" "What city are they in?" "What does the Bible say happened just before this picture?" "What does the Bible say happened after this picture?" "What are the people in the picture saying to each other?" "What Bible book describes the event in this picture?"

After children have written three to five questions each, collect quiz papers and redistribute them randomly for children to answer individually or as a group; you may use the questions to play a team game of Tic-Tac-Toe.

The List Goes On...

Materials: A chair for each child, Post-it Notes, marker, Christmas cassette/CD and player.

Preparation: Place chairs in a large circle. Stick a numbered Post-it Note on each chair.

Procedure: Play the Christmas music as children walk in one direction around the chairs. When the music stops, each child sits in a chair. Call out a pair of numbers. Child in first numbered chair names one object associated with Christmas (snow, decorations, manger, star, etc.). Child in second numbered chair repeats the item. Play a second round and call out two different numbers. Child in first numbered chair names a second Christmas object; child in second numbered chair tells the complete list of items (two, so far). Continue playing, building the Christmas list as long as possible.

Name That Song!

Materials: Bible, index cards, felt pen, butcher paper and marker or chalkboard and chalk, pencils and drawing paper; optional—large sketch pad or flip chart with blank pages.

Preparation: Choose 10 to 12 Christmas songs your children are most likely to be familiar with and write the song titles on index cards—one title per card. Display blank butcher paper or chalkboard. Place drawing paper and pencils in central location.

Procedure: Brainstorm Christmas song titles with children. Read aloud appropriate Bible verses (Luke 2:4; Luke 2:6,7; Luke 2:14; Matthew 2:2) to help children think of songs. List each song title that is suggested on butcher paper. Be sure that all titles from the index cards you prepared appear on the butcher paper list.

Each child then takes an index card and chooses one of three ways to make the class guess the song title: (1) hum the first few notes of the song; (2) draw a picture of what the song talks about; or (3) pantomime the title or action of the song. Children may refer to the list while guessing song titles. Remind them that there may be more titles on the butcher paper than you have written on the index cards. (Optional: Children use large sketch pad or flip chart sheets for drawing.)

Christmas Favorites

Materials: Large sheet of paper and marker or chalkboard and chalk, lightweight object such as a soft foam ball.

Preparation: Think of several categories that relate to the Christmas season such as favorite foods, songs, activities, etc.

Procedure: Have group sit in a circle. Discuss Christmas categories you thought of beforehand. Have children help you think of additional Christmas categories. List suggested categories on paper or chalkboard. Say the name of one of the categories while tossing a ball or other lightweight object to a child. The child must immediately name a favorite item that falls within that category. Then the child tosses the object to someone else who must also name something within the category. A child may change the category at any time by naming a new category while tossing the object to someone else. The person who receives the object must name something within the new category. The group should try to keep the object moving as quickly as possible to keep the game going.

After playing for a while, stop the object and hold it. Then point to a child in the circle. Ask the rest of the group what they remember about that person's Christmas favorites. Point to another child and continue until all children have been chosen. This is a fun way to help everyone get better acquainted!

Tell the News

Materials: Masking tape, paper, pencils.

Preparation: Place two lengths of masking tape 15 feet (4.5 m) apart to make a start line and a finish line.

Procedure: Ask children for seven key words from the Christmas story (e.g., "angel," "shepherds," "star," "baby," "Bethlehem," "good news," "Messiah"). List words on paper.

Divide children into two teams. Give each team a paper and pencils. Each team writes four newspaper articles as if they were alive and on the scene at the time of Jesus' birth. The four articles could be titled "Overcrowding Due to Roman Census," "Ancient Writing Puzzles Scholars," "Sky-High Performance," and "Born in a Barn." They must use each of the seven key words at least once. Collect papers. Teams line up behind the start line.

Place each team's papers at the finish line directly across from the opposing team. Call out a key word. First child in line runs to the finish line, finds the key word in the opposite team's newspaper, brings it back to the team and reads aloud the sentence in which the word is found before returning the newspaper to the finish line. Game continues until each team member has had at least one turn. To keep down the noise level, have children mime cheers for their teams. Give some examples of silent cheers such as jumping with arms raised or mouthing the words "go, go, go" while silently clapping. This mime of enthusiasm will be a fun part of the game!

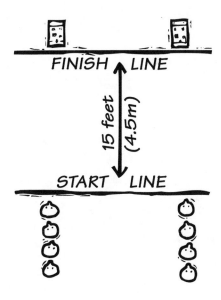

FINISH LINE

15 feet (4.5m)

START LINE

Activities

Activity Tips

The activities on these pages offer a variety of ways to help children explore the wonderful truths of the Christmas story. The hands-on experience of relating to biblical truth through drama, art, music or writing makes for powerful learning.

- Acting out the part of Mary or Joseph can help children remember the Christmas story far better than merely listening to even the best storyteller. Role-playing situations help children to concretely express abstract concepts like love, friendliness and sharing.

- Drawing and painting allow children to express thoughts or feelings that may be difficult to put into words and help them visualize specific actions to apply to Bible truths.
- Singing songs helps children memorize Scripture, learn Bible truths and experience moments of excitement and quietness.
- Writing can help children organize what they are learning as well as give them an opportunity to express what they think and feel about God or about their own experiences and needs.

Use these activities as springboards to bring the wonderful truths of Christmas home to your children.

- Know the learning purpose of each activity. Be able to explain *why* you are doing the activity, not just *what* you are doing.
- Guide the conversation during the activity to accomplish that purpose.
- Near the end of the activity, have your kids put into their own words what they have learned.

Star Path

Materials: Star Path Star Pattern, yellow construction paper, pencil, scissors, masking tape, incense, bottle of cologne, stones sprayed gold color.

Preparation: Use pattern to make 20 to 30 stars from construction paper. Tape stars to floor in an interesting path, ending at a point out of sight from the first star. Set incense, cologne and stones at end of path.

Procedure: Children follow the path of stars, moving in a variety of ways (hop, jump, walk backwards, etc.) to discover the items at the end of the path.

When Jesus was born, God made one star in the sky shine brighter than all the other stars around it. Some wise men followed that special star to find Jesus. They traveled for a long, long time. When they found Jesus, they gave Him special gifts like the ones you found.

Activities • Early Childhood
Count-the-Days December Calendar

Materials: Page for one month from a calendar with large numerals, scissors, a 2x3-foot (.6x.9-m) sheet of paper, felt pen, ruler, glue, crayons.

Preparation: Cut each day's numeral from the calendar page. (If calendar is unavailable, draw large numerals on paper and cut apart.) Draw a calendar grid on paper, sizing the boxes to accommodate the numerals cut from the calendar. Glue the numeral "1" in the appropriate space for the first day of December.

Procedure: Children arrange and glue remaining numerals to make a December calendar. Lightly color any days that have already passed. Color December 25 red. Decorate calendar edges. Help children count the days that remain until Christmas.

Why does Christmas make you so happy? Our Bible tells us that God sent Jesus because He loves us. Christmas shows us how much God loves us.

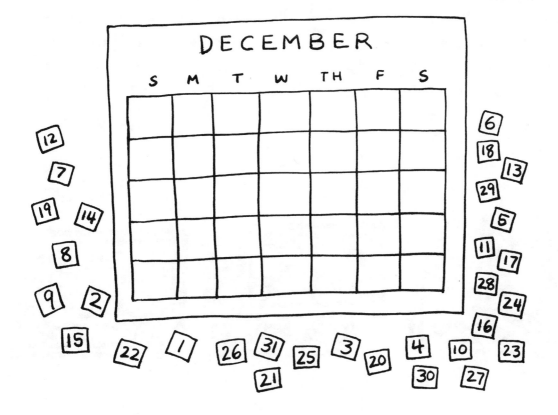

Match the Gifts

Materials: Scissors, wrapping paper in several patterns and colors, glue, index cards, bag or other container; optional—colored felt-tip pens.

Preparation: Cut two rectangles (smaller than index cards) from each pattern of wrapping paper. Glue each shape onto a separate index card. (Optional: Draw matching bows on each pair of "rectangles" to make them look like gifts.)

Procedure: Use the cards to play the following matching games with children:

1. Match Me. Give each child a card, keeping the matching card for yourself. Show your cards, one at a time, helping child with matching card to identify it.

2. Grab Bag Match. Place one set of cards faceup on floor or table. Place second set of cards in bag. Each child takes a card from the bag and finds the matching card on the floor or table.

3. Hide 'n' Seek Match. Hide all cards around the room. Children find cards and place them faceup on table or floor. Children take turns finding two matching cards.

Our cards look like gifts. It's fun to give gifts at Christmastime. Our Bible tells us that some wise men gave gifts to Jesus. The wise men gave Jesus gifts because they were glad He had been born.

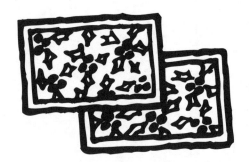

Thank-You Puzzles

Materials: Front panels from Christmas cards that show scenes of Jesus' birth, scissors, resealable plastic sandwich bags or envelopes for keeping puzzle pieces.

Procedure: Invite children to choose a card front and cut it into six to eight pieces to make a puzzle. Child rearranges pieces to put puzzle together. As children work, talk about what makes Christmas special.

We're happy at Christmastime because that's when we celebrate Jesus' birth. We're glad God sent Jesus to earth. You can tell God, "Thank You for sending Jesus" every time you make your puzzle.

Shepherds' Surprise Story Play

Procedure: Play out the story action with your child. Read the poem aloud and follow directions in italics.

Shepherds sit out on a hill.	*Sit in a circle.*
The sky is dark! It's night!	
The sheep are sleepy, lying still.	*Pretend to be a sleepy sheep.*
And then the sky gets bright!	*Shade eyes.*
"Don't be afraid," the angel says.	*Smile and shake head no.*
"I've got good news to sing!	
Today in Bethlehem is born	
The Son of God—the King!"	*Point upward.*
"You'll know the baby easily;	
He's sleeping in a barn.	*Pretend to be sleeping baby.*
He's wrapped and lying in the hay	*Hug yourself.*
To keep Him safe and warm."	
Then many other angels come	*Move fingers to show many.*
To praise God with a song;	
When they are gone, the shepherds say,	
"Let's go! It won't take long!"	*Look at each other.*
The shepherds run and soon they find	*Pretend to run.*
The quiet little barn.	
They see the baby Jesus there,	
Sleeping safe and warm.	*Pretend to rock a baby.*

Jesus' Birthday Mural

Materials: Shelf or butcher paper, marker, masking tape, used Christmas cards with both biblical and non-biblical illustrations, scissors.

Preparation: Letter paper as shown and tape to the wall.

Procedure: Sort cards with children by asking them what the pictures on the various cards show about Christmas. Keep only cards that picture something about Jesus' birthday. As you select cards, ask simple questions about the different ways birthdays are celebrated. Help children focus on how members of their families show God's love to them by helping them, caring for them, etc. Children tape cards to mural. (You may want children to trim pictures before attaching them to mural.)

We celebrate Christmas because it is Jesus' birthday. Jesus' birthday shows us how much God loves us. This "Happy Birthday" mural helps us say, "Thank You, God, for sending us Jesus."

Wise Men's Gifts

Materials: Frankincense, myrrh-scented incense, matches, small metal or stoneware dish for incense, stones sprayed gold color.

Preparation: If practical, begin burning incense in metal or stoneware dish (out of children's reach) before children arrive.

Procedure: Children examine gold stones and smell the incense. Allow time for children to react to the sights and smells.

Have you ever taken a gift to a new baby? Our Bible tells about some gifts that wise men brought to little Jesus. This pretend gold looks like one of those gifts. Another gift was like this frankincense. How do you think it smells? The wise men also brought Jesus incense like this. How do you think it smells? The wise men gave wonderful gifts to Jesus when He was born because they knew He was God's Son.

Decorate a Tree

Materials: Small artificial Christmas tree, tree stand, unbreakable tree ornaments, ornament hangers.

Preparation: Secure the tree in stand and place on low table or floor.

Procedure: Children decorate the tree with ornaments while talking about ways people show love to each other and ways God shows His love to us. Resist the temptation to take over the tree-decorating project. It may not meet adult standards, but the tree should make each child proud. Each child should feel, *I helped decorate our tree!*

What a beautiful tree! I like the way you are decorating it. What are your favorite tree decorations? Sometimes people put gifts under their Christmas trees. God gave us the very best gift ever. Our Bible tells us that God loves us and sent His Son, Jesus.

Musical Glasses

Materials: Several glasses, large pitcher of water, small measuring cup with pouring spout, spoons.

Procedure: Guide children to fill glasses with different levels of water. Children gently tap glasses with spoons to hear the sounds.

What do these sounds remind you of? These sounds remind me of bells. Let's pretend you're ringing Christmas bells. Why do we like to make happy sounds like these at Christmas time? Listen carefully to comments. Acknowledge each comment with a nod or a smile.

Christmas is when we celebrate Jesus' birthday. I'm glad God kept His promise to send Jesus. It makes me feel like ringing these Christmas bells again! Allow children to empty, refill and rearrange glasses from lowest to highest sounds and experiment with the different tones.

Nativity Scene Talk

Materials: Unbreakable nativity scene with figures.

Procedure: As children take turns arranging the figures in the scene, identify each figure and talk with children about God's promise to send His Son, Jesus.

These people remind us of the special time that Jesus was born. This woman is Mary. Mary was Jesus' mother. The Bible tells us that God sent an angel to talk to Mary. The angel said that Mary would have a baby. Her baby would be God's Son. Mary was glad! Do you know the baby's name? Allow children to respond. Proceed through the figures in your nativity set as time and interest permit. Lead children in prayer, thanking God for each part of the Christmas story.

Rhythm Sticks

Materials: Red and green construction paper, tape, Christmas carol cassette/CD and player; optional—two small jingle bells for each child, stapler.

Preparation: Make a sample set of rhythm sticks, rolling and taping two sheets of paper as shown.

Procedure: Demonstrate use of the rhythm sticks. Help each child roll and tape two sheets of paper to make rhythm sticks. (Optional: Child inserts bell into each rhythm stick. Help child staple ends of sticks closed.) Children tap rhythm sticks together as you play Christmas music on the cassette/CD player.

We are glad that God sent His Son, Jesus. One of the ways we can show we are glad is to make music. Let's tap our sticks together to the music. Making music to God is a way to say thank-you to Him.

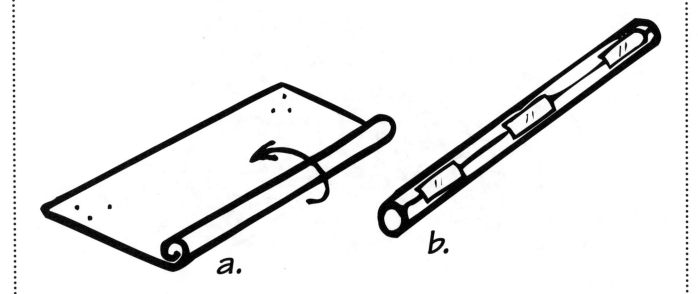

a.

b.

Who Loves Jesus?

Who loves little baby Jesus?

His mother, Mary, loved Him.

Joseph loved Him.

The shepherds loved Him.

The wise men loved Him.

And I love Him.

Do you love Him, too?

Look in the Stable

Let's look into the stable now.

Who do you see inside?

I see baby Jesus sleeping,

Mary and Joseph nearby.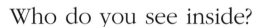

Count.

Jesus sleeps but has no crib.

He sleeps on the hay.

Jesus has no fancy clothes.

He's wrapped in cloth this way.

Bring an unbreakable nativity set to class, along with a doll wrapped in strips of cloth for "swaddling clothes."
Invite children to wrap eard unwrap the doll.

The First Christmas

Here is kind Joseph

And here is sweet Mary.

She rode and he walked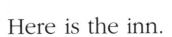

On their Bethlehem journey.

Ride. Walk in place.

Here is the inn.

Joseph knocked at the door, Knock.

But each bed was full;

There was no room for more.  Shake head, no.

They were both tired; Yawn.

It was late in the day,

So they went to the stable

To sleep on the hay.

And there in the stable

That first Christmas morn,

Jesus our Savior,

God's own Son, was born.  Rock baby.

Ring the Bells

Ring, ring, ring the bells,
Ring them loud and clear
To tell the people everywhere
That Christmas time is here.

Clap, clap, clap your hands,
Clap them loud and clear
To tell the people everywhere
That Christmas time is here.

Stamp, stamp, stamp your feet,
Stamp them loud and clear
To tell the people everywhere
That Christmas time is here.

Instant Song: Sing to the tune of "Row, Row, Row Your Boat."

Jesus' Birthday

It's Jesus' birthday—

Time to sing!

Shake the bells

To make them ring.

Let's all sing a happy song.

Bring your (drums)

And march along!

Invite children to name other instruments (trumpets, tambourines, bells, etc.). Form a parade and repeat the poem, naming each instrument suggested.

Christmas Time

The snow is falling softly down;

The fire is burning warm.

 Warm hands.

Let's decorate the Christmas tree

And say "Thank You!" to the Lord.

I hear someone in the kitchen.

I smell cookies baking there!

We'll sing a song to Jesus,

Let our music fill the air!

 Sniff.

The Shepherds

Some shepherds took care of their sheep,

Out on the hills that night,

When suddenly they saw a light

So very, very bright.

An angel said, "Don't be afraid.

I've news for everyone.

Tonight a baby boy was born.

This baby is God's Son."

The shepherds ran to Bethlehem

To see if this was true.

And there they saw God's special gift

To them—to me—and you!

It's Christmas

It's Christmas! It's Christmas!

The Christmas bells ring—

The birthday of Jesus,

Our Savior and King.

It's Christmas! It's Christmas!

The Christmas stars shine—

The birthday of Jesus,

A glad, happy time!

It's Christmas! It's Christmas!

The candles all glow—

The birthday of Jesus,

Let everyone know.

It's Christmas! It's Christmas!

Our Bible recalls

The birthday of Jesus,

God's love gift to all.

Snowflakes

Snowflakes fall as soft as kittens.

See! I catch them on my mittens.

Now I crunch them with my feet.

Slip and slide on snowy streets.

Child colors the pictures and circles the pictures that tell about how Jesus was born.

Name _____

Who took care of baby Jesus when He was born? Who takes care of you?

Christmas Crafts and Activities © 1998 by Gospel Light. Permission to photocopy granted.

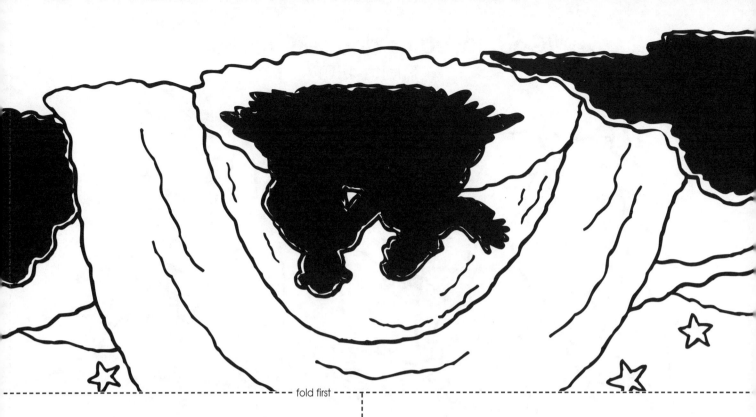

- - - - - - - - - - - - - - - - - - fold first -

To: _____

From: _____

Child colors card. Child then folds as indicated. Letter names
on this page. (Optional: Child glues wisps of cotton to sheep.)

Christmas Crafts and Activities © 1998 by Gospel Light. Permission to photocopy granted.   123

"(God) loved us and sent His Son."
(1 John 4:10)

Christmas Crafts and Activities

thanks

name

Prefold page. Child colors pictures and refolds page. Child opens flaps and names items to thank God for. **What do you see under this flap? Who is a friend you are thankful for?** (Optional: Child completes page without folding it.)

Name _____

Child opens flaps.

fold forward

fold forward

fold forward

fold forward

for

God

"It is good to give thanks to the Lord."

Psalm 92:1 *(NASB)*

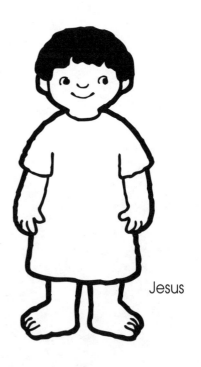

Jesus

"The Lord
your God
is with you."
Zephaniah 3:17

Side 2

Cut slit on line between dots.   fold

Side 1

cut

Tape here.

fold

127

Beforehand, cut a slit on the line between dots. Child colors page, cuts off star strip, folds page and strip and tapes strip. Child slides strip into precut slit. **Why did God put a special star in the sky? What did King Herod tell the wise men? What did God tell the wise men in a dream?**

Name: _____

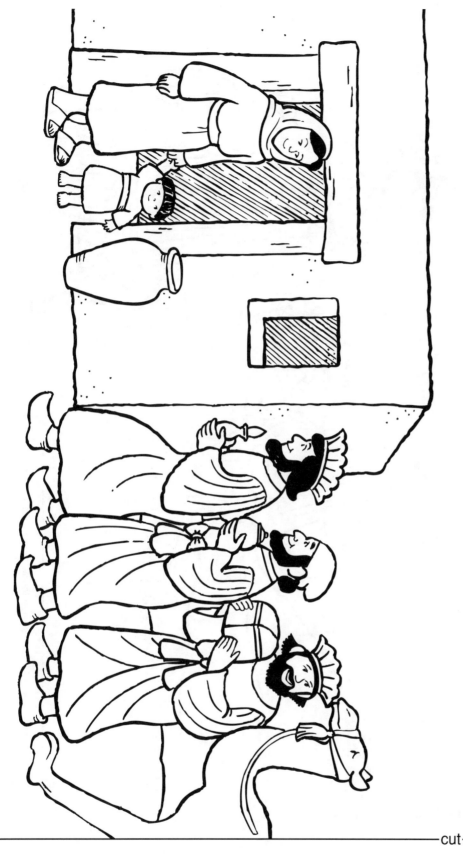

Beforehand, cut slit in page above house. Child colors picture and then cuts off star. Child tapes star to top of craft stick. Help child place craft stick in slit so star rests above the house. (Optional: Child glues gold paper on gift of gold and dabs cotton swab dipped in perfume on gift of myrrh.) **God was with the wise men to help them find Jesus. God is with you, too.**

"God is with you." Zephaniah 3:17

cut

cut

Name _____

Child colors page. **What did the wise men follow to find Jesus? Who put the star in the sky?**

cut

Tape craft stick here.

cut

Christmas Crafts and Activities © 1998 by Gospel Light. Permission to photocopy granted.

Would you like to see

the gifts the wise men brought to Jesus?

Would You Like to See?

staple

staple

---

fold

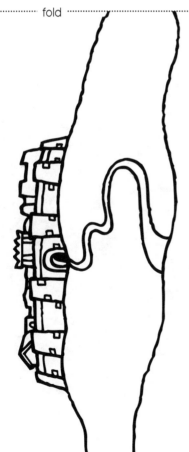

Would you like to see

the city where the wise men talked to King Herod?

"Be glad in the Lord."
(See Psalm 32:11.)

Name _____

Child colors scenes and then cuts and folds as indicated.
Child staples book and then tapes top edge of a paper
square over each picture on pages 2-7. Child reads the book,
lifting paper square on each page.

Tape

Would you like to see

who the wise men came to visit?

6

Would you like to see

the star that led the wise men to Jesus?

2

Would you like to see

how the wise men traveled?

3

Would you like to see

what the wise men did when they saw Jesus?

7

cut

Tape along this edge

cut

Tape bottom of angel figure here.

cut

Tape along this edge.

What did the angel tell the shepherds?

Name: _____

Scene 1

What did the shepherds do? Who did God plan to care for baby Jesus? Who did God plan to care for you?

Tape stable door here.

Child colors pictures and then cuts on lines and tapes angel figure to Scene 1 and stable door to Scene 2 where indicated. (Optional: Child glues cotton to sheep and adds stars to sky.)

"(God) loved us and sent his Son." 1 John 4:10

cut

cut

Child colors pictures and names person to whom card will be sent. Child cuts and folds card. Child glues gummed stars to nighttime sky and cotton to sheep.

"(God) loved us and sent his Son." 1 John 4:10

5

cut — fold

fold 2

Jesus Is Born!

To: _____

From: _____

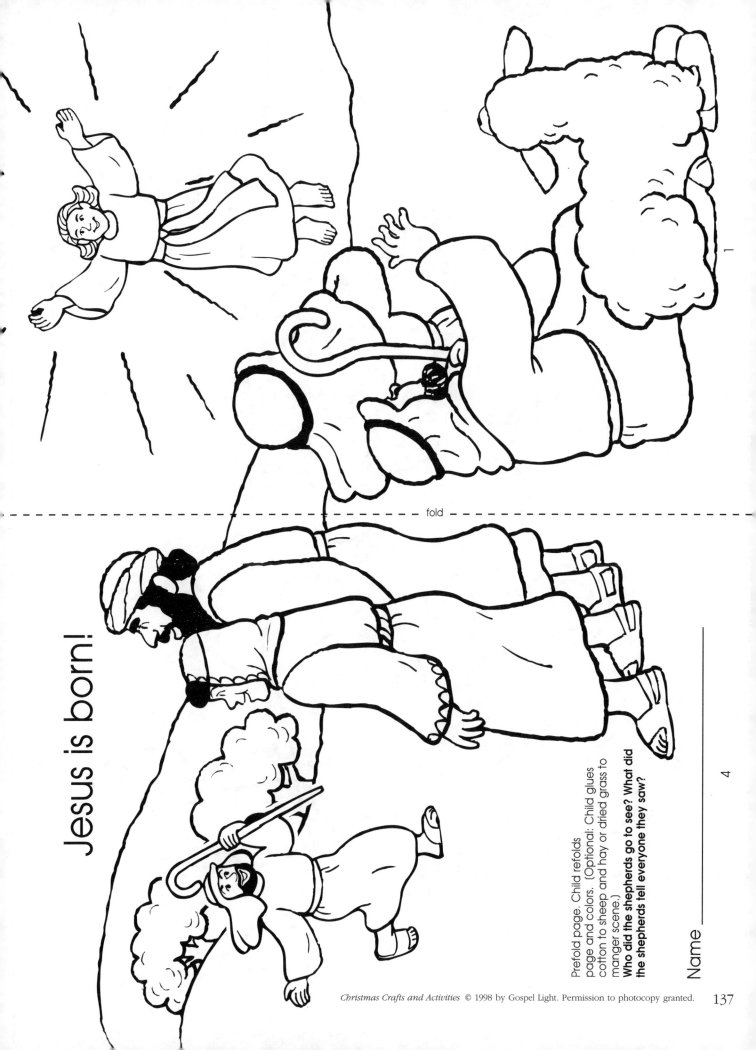

Jesus is born!

fold

1

4

Prefold page. Child refolds
page and colors. (Optional: Child glues
cotton to sheep and hay or dried grass to
manger scene.)
**Who did the shepherds go to see? What did
the shepherds tell everyone they saw?**

Name _____

Christmas Crafts and Activities © 1998 by Gospel Light. Permission to photocopy granted.   137

Christmas Crafts and Activities © 1998 by Gospel Light. Permission to photocopy granted.

God loved us and sent the Lord Jesus.

(See 1 John 4:10.)

fold forward

Prefold page. Child folds and colors page. **Jesus is God's gift to us. What is a kind thing to say when you receive a present?** Lead child in a brief thank-you prayer to God. (Optional: Child glues ribbon to gift.)

Name _____

fold forward

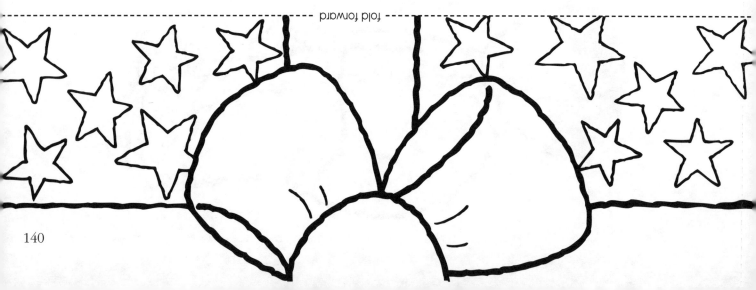

"God loved us  and sent His Son,  "Jesus." (See 1 John 4:10.)

2

— fold first —

Tape

— fold second —

Good News!

To: _____

From: _____

3

1

Prefold page. Child refolds page to make a card. Ask child to whom he or she wishes to give the card. Write names on page 1. Child colors pages. Child tapes wrapping paper to cover picture of baby Jesus on page 3.

Here is the inn.
Joseph knocked
at the door,

But each bed was full;
There was no room
for more.

cut

Here is kind Joseph
and here is
sweet Mary.

fold first

STAPLE

STAPLE

fold

They were both tired; It was late in the day.
So they went to the stable to sleep on the hay.

cut

Child colors pictures and adds Sticker 1. Optional: Child tapes twine for donkey's rope, glues straw in stable and adds gummed stars to sky. **Where did Mary and Joseph go? Where did they sleep? What did they do to care for baby Jesus? How does your family care for you?**

Child cuts and folds where indicated, then places one section inside the other so page numbers are consecutive. Assist with stapler.

Name _____

Christmas Crafts and Activities © 1998 by Gospel Light. Permission to photocopy granted.

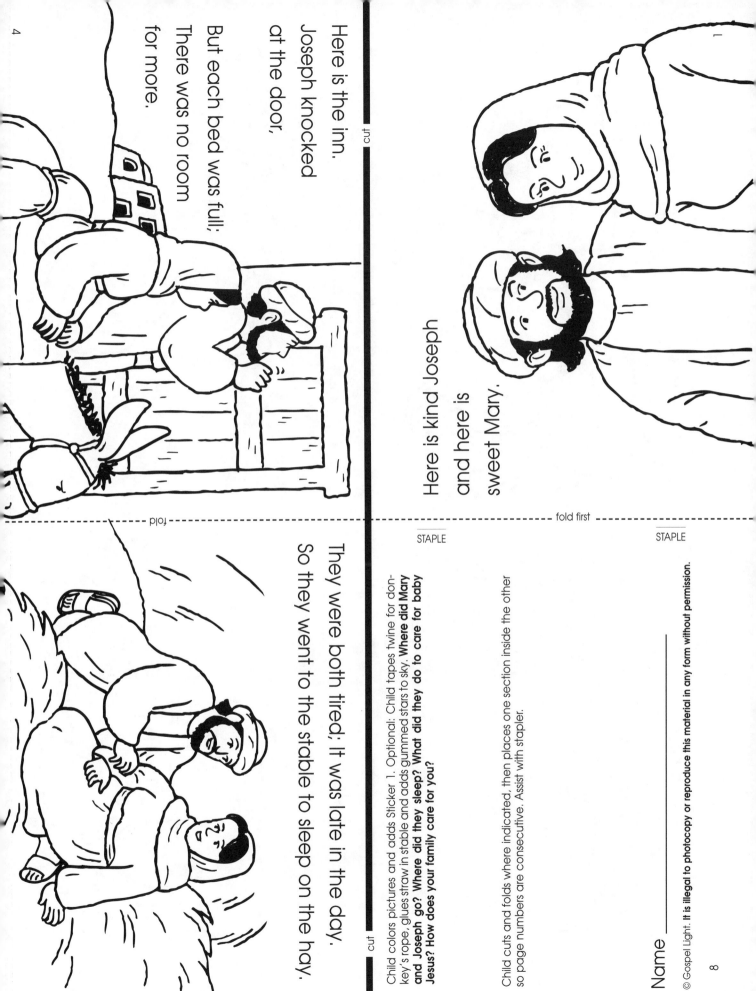

2

She rode
and he walked

on their Bethlehem journey,

3

And there in the stable
That first Christmas morn,

9

God cared for Jesus.
"(God) cares for you." (1 Peter 5:7)

Jesus our Savior,
God's own Son, was born.

7

cut

fold

fold

cut

Christmas Crafts and Activities © 1998 by Gospel Light. Permission to photocopy granted.

Child colors picture. **Who told the shepherds good news? How did the shepherds feel when they saw the angel?**

Name _____

Navtivity Scene

Child colors figures and then cuts figures apart. Child glues figures to paper to make a nativity scene.

It is good to sing to our God. (See Psalm 147:1.)

Child colors the path to find Jesus. **What did the shepherds do after the angel left? What did the shepherds tell God?**

Child colors picture. **What did God do to keep Jesus safe from the mean king? Who cared for Jesus?** (Optional: Child adds star stickers to nighttime sky.)

It's a Wrap

Materials: Bible, Christmas wrapping paper, ruler, scissors, felt pen, paper, tape.

Preparation: Letter the words of Luke 2:11 on the backs of 3x5-inch (7.5x12.5-cm) rectangles cut from wrapping paper—two or three words on each rectangle. (Challenge: Write each word on a separate rectangle.) Letter entire verse on another sheet of paper and tape paper where all can see it.

Procedure: Place rectangles, colored side up, on floor in random order. Children work together to turn over rectangles and place words in correct order, referring to the verse written on paper. Read Luke 2:11 together, guiding children to jump up and say "Hurray!" at the end of the verse. Discuss why Jesus' birth in Bethlehem was such good news. Repeat process several times, allowing volunteers to mix up the words. (Challenge: Remove paper on which Luke 2:11 is lettered. Children put words in order from memory.)

Christmas Song Chart

Materials: Butcher paper, markers, Christmas carol cassette/CD and player.

Preparation: Letter words of a Christmas song from the cassette/CD on butcher paper, leaving space to draw pictures under them.

Procedure: Play the song on cassette/CD player and encourage children to sing along, using the words from the chart. Ask questions to bring out the meaning of the words and how they reflect God's love in sending His Son. Lay butcher paper chart on table or floor and distribute markers. Play song on cassette as children illustrate the words on the chart. Ask two children to hold up the completed word chart so everyone can see it. Divide group into two teams and have teams stand facing each other. First team sings a line and second team echoes the line. (Optional: Allow children to display their word chart and sing the song for parents, another group of children, etc.)

Picture God's Plan Rebus

Materials: Bible, length of butcher paper, felt pens.

Preparation: Letter the words of John 3:16a on butcher paper, leaving large spaces for the words "loved," "world," "gave" and "Son." (See sketch a.)

Procedure: Read or quote John 3:16a aloud and then spread butcher paper on table or floor. Invite children to read John 3:16a from butcher paper, filling in the missing words from memory. Explain that Jesus' birth was something God planned a long time ago. Discuss what the verse says about God's plan for His Son and for us.

Ask volunteers to suggest ways to picture the words that are missing in the verse ("loved"—heart; "world"—globe, people of different races and ages; "gave"—outstretched hand, gift; "Son"—Jesus, baby in a manger). Children work together in pairs or small groups to illustrate the missing words (see sketch b). Children may draw more than one picture for each missing word. One child in each group may write the missing word.

God's plan was to send Jesus to earth so everyone could see what God is like and become members of His family. Where can we put our poster so that lots of people will read it and know about God's plan? If possible, have children help you display the poster in a visible location at your church.

a.

b.

Personal Favorites

Materials: Christmas wrapping paper, ruler, pencil, scissors, white paper, tape, felt pens.

Preparation: Cut wrapping paper into 5-inch (12.5-cm) squares—two for each child.

Procedure: Distribute one sheet of white paper and two wrapping paper squares to each child. Children tape tops of squares onto paper. Instruct them to draw a picture of a present they would like to receive under one square and a picture of a present they would like to give to someone under the other. Volunteers show and describe their completed drawings or give clues to help others guess the gifts before showing their drawings.

It's fun to get something you've always wanted or needed. The Bible talks about a very special gift that God gave us at Christmas—the gift of His Son, Jesus. Jesus came to show us what God is like and to make a way for us to become members of God's family. Jesus is the best Christmas present we could ever receive—or give to others!

Christmas Crafts and Activities © 1998 by Gospel Light. Permission to photocopy granted.

Eyewitness News

Materials: Name tags, felt pen, aluminum foil, cardboard tube, transparent tape.

Preparation: Make a name tag for each character in the Christmas story—Mary, Joseph, innkeeper, villagers and shepherds. Make enough name tags for villagers and shepherds so that each child will have a part. Roll a 5-inch (12.5-cm) square of aluminum foil into a ball. Tape foil ball to the top of the cardboard tube to use as a pretend microphone.

Procedure: Explain that reporters often interview eyewitnesses to get information for their reports and that an eyewitness is someone who actually saw an event happen. Ask for volunteers to be "eyewitnesses" to the Christmas story. Give children the appropriate name tags to wear. You play the part of the reporter and interview each character or group of characters to find out what happened when Jesus was born. **Mary, how did you feel when you first saw the angel? What did the angel tell you? What did you think of what the angel told you? Joseph, why did you and Mary travel to Bethlehem? What did you think when there was no room for you? Innkeeper, why did you tell Mary and Joseph to stay in the stable? Why was the town so crowded? Shepherds, how did you feel when you first saw the angel? What did the angels say to you? What did you do when you first saw Jesus? What did you do to show you were glad Jesus was born? Villagers, what did the shepherds tell you? Did you believe them? Why or why not?**

After the interviews, allow children to tell their favorite parts of the Christmas story. They may also tell how they plan to celebrate Jesus' birth with their families.

Enhancement ideas:

1. Use Bible-times costumes.

2. Tape-record or videotape interviews and play them back to the group or incorporate them into a Christmas program or celebration.

3 Let children pretending to be shepherds, villagers and innkeeper think of names for themselves.

4. Bring several Bible-times books showing pictures of inns, stables and shepherds to show to children.

Gifts of Love

Materials: Marker, large sheet of butcher paper, Christmas wrapping paper, scissors, tape or glue, paper, felt pens; optional—ribbon or yarn bows.

Preparation: Letter "This is how God showed His love among us" across the top of the butcher paper. From the wrapping paper, cut out gift package shapes slightly larger than the papers you will give children to draw on; with decorated side facing out, tape or glue by top edge only to butcher paper. (Optional: Attach bows to top of each "gift" on tape or glue line.)

Procedure: Discuss with children why we give gifts to each other at Christmas. Explain that God also gives us gifts because He loves us but that His gifts don't always come wrapped in boxes with pretty bows. Ask volunteers to name some gifts God gives us. Children draw pictures of gifts from God on paper and tape or glue their pictures under the wrapping paper "packages." Allow volunteers to share their drawings and then pray, thanking God for each gift of love He has given.

Good News Angel Puzzle

Materials: Bible, paper or lightweight cardboard, felt pen, scissors; optional—resealable plastic bags.

Preparation: Cut a large angel shape from paper or cardboard (see sketch). Write the angel's words from Luke 2:10 on one side of the angel. Cut angel into puzzle pieces. (Optional: Make a puzzle for each child and put puzzle pieces in bags.)

Procedure: Children put puzzle pieces together to form angel. Read the verse aloud. Invite the children to read the verse together with you. Explain that these are the words an angel told the shepherds on the night Jesus was born. Talk about the shepherds' joyful response to the angel's good news—they praised God and told everyone they saw that Jesus had been born. Ask volunteers to name ways they can tell others the good news today and then pray, thanking God for the good news about His Son.

(Challenge: Write Luke 2:11 on the back of the angel before cutting apart. Children can mix up the pieces and turn them over before assembling a second time to "hear" the rest of the angel's good news.)

"Do not be afraid. I bring you good news of great joy that will be for all the people." Luke 2:10

"You Were There" Pantomime

Materials: Large sheet of paper and marker or chalkboard and chalk, construction paper, scissors, glue, transparent tape, stapler and staples, hole punch, yarn.

Preparation: Decide whether you want to pantomime the entire Christmas story or only portions of it. Small groups may still act out the whole story by changing parts and costumes for each story section.

Procedure: Explain that a pantomime is a play that is done with actions but without words. Ask children to tell the events of the Christmas story in order. List events on paper or chalkboard. Ask for a volunteer to be the narrator who will read the story from the list. Assign other children parts to play in the pantomime. Parts might include Mary, Joseph, innkeeper, shepherds, angel, wise men, King Herod and soldiers.

Children use construction paper to make costumes and props (i.e., hat or belt) or simple name cards to identify the character being played. As narrator reads the events of the story from paper or chalkboard, children act out parts.

If possible, have the children share their pantomime with a group of younger children, with their parents or in a worship service.

Christmas Crafts and Activities © 1998 by Gospel Light. Permission to photocopy granted.

Family Advent Calendar

Materials: Family Advent Calendar Pattern, photocopier, paper, one 10x12-inch (25x30-cm) sheet of red or white construction paper for each child, scissors, tape, crayons, pencils or fine-tip felt pens, world map.

Preparation: Duplicate Family Advent Calendar Pattern on plain paper—one for each child, plus several extras. Cut windows, door and triangle shapes from two of these extra copies to use as patterns. Complete a sample calendar following the instructions below.

Procedure: Explain the following: Advent is the season before Christmas when Christians prepare to celebrate Jesus' coming into the world. An Advent calendar is a picture calendar that has paper "doors" to open for each day of December until Christmas Day. Behind each paper door there is usually a picture or words about Jesus' birthday. Show sample Advent calendar you made.

Distribute one sheet of construction paper to each child. Show the photocopied patterns you cut. Help children center the cut patterns on construction paper and outline the shapes with a pencil (see sketch a). Children may then cut along three sides of each shape (see sketch b).

Give each child an uncut Advent Calendar Pattern. Position the construction paper over the calendar pattern so that the writing behind each shape can be seen. Turn pages over. Fold the edges of the construction paper over the edges of the calendar pattern and tape down (sketch c). Children may decorate the front of calendars (sketch d).

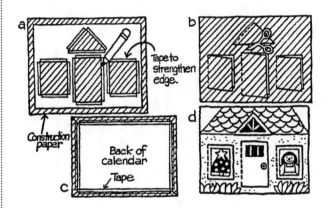

Explain that people all over the world celebrate Jesus' birthday. In other countries, families do different things to celebrate Jesus' birth. Volunteers locate on map the countries mentioned on calendar (Sweden, Mexico, Australia and the Philippines). Read and discuss the instructions on calendar for each activity with children. Encourage children to do these activities with their families one night each week until Christmas.

Activities • **Lower Elementary**
Family Advent Calendar Pattern

SWEDEN
Decorate the house with a brightly colored frieze (a series of pictures on a long strip of paper).
You need: butcher paper and crayons, felt pens or paints.
To do: Decide what you will draw—the Christmas story or ways your family celebrates Christmas. Plan who will draw each scene. Have fun!

PHILIPPINES
As the people of the Philippines do, remember the birds. Place bread or cracker crumbs on shrubs and trees outdoors.

AUSTRALIA
Decorate the house with flowers—it's spring in Australia!
You need: real flowers, vases. Or make paper flowers (see instructions below). Place flowers in as many rooms as possible.
To make paper flowers: Cut flower petals from construction paper. Glue to one end of ice cream stick.

MEXICO
Act out the Posadas Festival. (Posadas means a place to live.)
You need: a nativity scene (objects or picture), two candles (or flashlights).
To do: Choose two family members to be Mary and Joseph. Place nativity scene in one room. At night, "Mary" and "Joseph" hold lighted candles and walk from room to room looking for a place to stay. When they reach the room with nativity scene, they stop and place candles by it.

Newspaper Search for Peace

Materials: Newspapers (one news section for each pair of children), scissors.

Procedure: Group children in pairs. Each pair finds and cuts out newspaper articles or pictures about situations in which people need peace. Lead children to describe and discuss their articles by asking questions, such as, **Who are the people who need peace in this article? What problem are they having? What might someone do to make peace in this situation? What are some ways that Jesus helps people make peace? What might groups of people at school who don't get along do to make peace? What might family members do to be peacemakers with each other?**

Preparing for Christmas

Materials: Bibles, large sheet of butcher paper, red and green markers, tape, Post-it Notes or index cards.

Preparation: On butcher paper, draw two large intersecting circles or wreaths, one in each color. Tape paper to wall.

Procedure: Give several Post-it Notes or cards to each child. Lead children to think of ways they may prepare for Christmas (Decorate a tree. Send cards. Give gifts to others. Obey Jesus. Thank God for sending Jesus to be born. Collect canned goods or other donations for charitable groups. Set up manger scene. Sing Christmas carols.) Working alone or in pairs, children write each idea on a separate note or card.

Then refer to the two circles. Explain that in the red circle children will place notes or cards that tell ways to prepare for Christmas with celebrations in their homes, schools, churches or towns. In the green circle, they will put ways to prepare for Christmas with attitudes and actions that show love for Jesus. In the section where both circles overlap, they will put ways to prepare for Christmas that do both. Volunteers read notes or cards aloud and place them in the appropriate sections of the circles. Discuss children's ideas for ways to prepare for Christmas by asking questions, such as, **Which of the ideas in the red circle does your family do? Which section of the circles has the most ideas in it? the least? What are some other ideas we could put in the section that has the least? Which of the ideas in the green circle have you done? Which way of preparing for Christmas is your favorite? Why? Which way of preparing for Christmas have you never done? Which new way of preparing for Christmas would you like to do this week?**

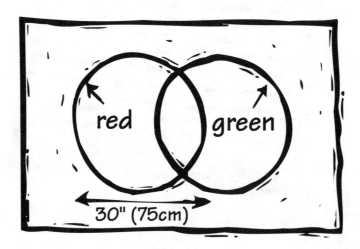

red   green

30" (75cm)

Spin the Light

Materials: Flashlight, index cards, marker.

Preparation: Letter discussion questions related to the Christmas story on separate index cards.

Procedure: Children sit in a circle. (Darken the room, if possible.) Turn on the flashlight and place it in the middle of the circle. Volunteer chooses and reads a question card and then spins the flashlight. When the flashlight stops, child closest to the beam of light from the flashlight answers the question. (Optional: Spin the flashlight for another child to answer the same question.)

Child who answered the question chooses and reads another question card and spins the flashlight. Continue with other questions as time permits.

Christmas Music Walkabout

Materials: Christmas music cassette/CD and player, 6-foot (1.8-m) lengths of butcher paper, markers.

Preparation: Choose a Christmas song found on the cassette/CD and write key phrases from that song on butcher paper. Prepare a copy of the paper for each group of six to eight children.

Procedure: Children form pairs. Place butcher paper on floor. Assign each pair one phrase from the Christmas carol. Allow several minutes for each pair to think of one question to ask other children about the assigned phrase ("Who was the first to hear about Jesus birth?" or "What did the angel say to the shepherds?"). Each pair takes a turn to read the assigned phrase and ask their question. Volunteers answer the questions.

Then place a marker or two by each phrase. As you play the Christmas carol, children walk around the paper. When you stop the music, each child finds a phrase to sit by. Each child draws an illustration or symbol representing the phrase on the paper. Repeat activity with other carols.

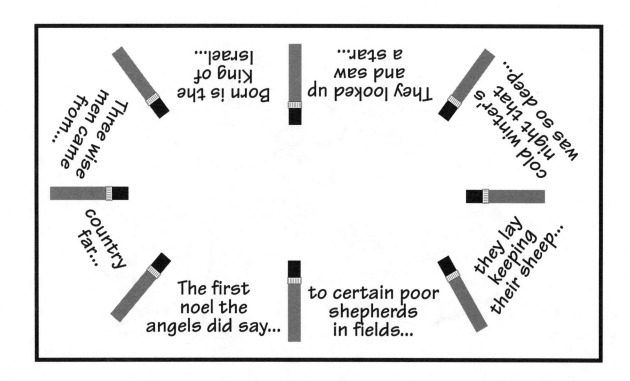

Christmas Giving Reminders

Materials: Butcher paper, marker, letter paper, pens, envelopes.

Preparation: Find out what giving projects your church or a local charitable organization has planned and how your group of children can participate. Choose one project for your group of children to support.

Procedure: Ask several volunteers to name things for which they are particularly thankful this Christmas. Talk about the many ways God meets our needs and takes care of us. Introduce the giving project planned by your church or a local charitable organization as a way to share God's love and kindness with others. Explain how children can participate. List on butcher paper any information children need to know about the giving project (items to be collected for donation, date by which the items need to be collected, instructions to follow, etc.). Then distribute letter paper, pens and envelopes to children. Each child writes a letter reminding the recipient to participate in the giving project. Children include information from butcher paper in their letters. Suggest that children also write the reason for the giving project. Each child addresses an envelope to him- or herself. If time permits, children may write a second letter to be sent to someone else the child hopes will participate in the giving project.

Collect letters and envelopes. During the week, mail the letters to children, making sure each child does not receive his or her own letter. On the appropriate date, collect items for the giving project and distribute them as needed.

The Wish List

Materials: Bibles, large sheet of butcher paper, marker.

Preparation: Divide paper in half by drawing a line from top to bottom. At the top of the left side, write "Wish List 1"; write "Wish List 2" at the top of the right side.

Procedure: Ask children to name items kids might have on a Christmas wish list. As each item is named, a volunteer writes these items in the first column, "Wish List 1." List 8 to 10 items. Then lead children to quickly vote on the likelihood of kids their age receiving each item: "will get," "won't get," "maybe will get." Write the number of votes each phrase receives next to each item on the list.

Then have children name gifts that Jesus gives to people (Peace. Joy. Counsel. Forgiveness. Salvation. Help. Comfort).

Children may refer to Isaiah 9:6,7 for ideas. A volunteer writes gifts in the second column, "Wish List 2."

Compare and discuss the two wish lists by asking questions, such as, **How does it feel when you expect to get something but don't get it? How does it feel to look forward to getting something good when you are certain of receiving it? How can Jesus' gift of (help) help kids your age? How could one of these gifts from Jesus help a kid who feels lonely and sad? help a kid who is angry because someone put him or her down? help a kid who doesn't know about being in God's family yet? What could prevent you from receiving the items on list 2?** Pray together, thanking God for the gifts He gives those who trust in Him.

Wish List 1   Wish List 2

Christmas TV Spots

Materials: Bibles, selection of Christmas items and Christmas carol songbooks, Christmas carol cassettes/CDs and player; optional—video recorder.

Procedure: Based on Biblical passages of the Christmas story, children create TV spots that remind us of the real story and meaning of Christmas. TV spots may incorporate Christmas items, carols and TV jingles. Each team of two or three children presents its spot to the rest of the children. (Optional: Videotape commercials to show at a party.)

Bible Verse Echoes

Materials: Bible, butcher paper, marker.

Preparation: Letter Luke 2:11 on butcher paper. Divide the verse into sections by using slash marks and then alternately number the sections "1" or "2."

Procedure: Children read Luke 2:11 together aloud. Ask questions to make sure children understand the words and the meaning of the verse. Divide children into two teams. Assign each team a number. Refer to verse divisions on butcher paper and have children read the phrases that match their team number. Practice saying the verse this way several times. Then add motions to the reading (e.g., stand to read your phrase and then sit down; raise hand and then lower it; cup hands to mouth and then remove them; etc.). Vary the activity by having Team 2 echo the phrases and repeat the movements of Team 1. Reverse team numbers periodically.

(1) (2)
Today / in the town /
(1) (2)
of David / a Savior /
(1) (2)
has been born / to you; /
(1) (2)
he is Christ / the Lord.
Luke 2:11

Christmas Carol Fun

Materials: Christmas songbooks and cassette/CD and player, large sheets of paper and markers or chalkboard and chalk, paper, pencils, felt pens, scissors, tape or thumbtacks.

Preparation: Letter the words to some of the Christmas carols on large sheets of paper or chalkboard.

Procedure: Encourage children to sing along as you play the Christmas carols. Ask questions to make sure children understand the words and meanings of the songs. Then do one of the following activities:

1. Distribute paper, pencils and felt pens. Allow children to create an illustration of their favorite Christmas carol.

2. Help children create a rebus chart—a poster on which pictures are used to replace some of the words—for one of the songs. They can use the chart to teach the song to another group of kids.

3. Make a Christmas banner to illustrate one of the carols. Cut a banner shape from a large sheet of paper. Letter the title of a Christmas carol on the banner, making one word of the title in large block letters. Place banner on a long table. Children work together in pairs or groups of three to fill in each block letter with words or pictures to describe the Christmas story. Attach banner to wall or bulletin board or give it to a local nursing home, hospital or shut-in person.

Bethlehem Walk

Materials: Materials for the craftspeople and activities you choose.

Preparation: Set up an area as a walk-through Bethlehem with different Bible-times craftspeople.

Procedure: Children visit "workrooms" of various craftspeople, learning about life in Bible times as they imagine what Mary and Joseph saw in Bethlehem the night they searched for a place to stay.

Suggested craftspeople and activities:

1. *Scribe:* Spread melted wax on cardboard tablets. Children use pencils or cuticle sticks to write on the wax tablets.

2. *Potter:* Provide clay for children to use to make clay lamps or bowls.

3. *Weaver:* Children weave small mats from paper or yarn.

4. *Baker:* Children make matzo bread.

5. *Carpenter:* Allow children to experiment with planing, chiseling and sawing wood, pounding a nail with a mallet and making holes with an awl or a drill.

Tree of Cards

Materials: Christmas tree, tree stand, strands of Christmas lights, Christmas carol cassette/CD and player, used Christmas cards, scissors, hole punch, yarn, tape or glue.

Preparation: Secure tree in stand and drape the lights on tree.

Procedure: Play Christmas carols as children use their imaginations to design and construct tree decorations from the cards. Children may simply cut out the illustrations or designs from the cards, punch holes in them and hang them on the tree with loops of yarn. They may cut Christmas shapes (stars, trees, crosses, balls, etc.) or characters (Jesus, Mary, angel, sheep, etc.) from the cards, or they may glue or tape a character to a shape. Children may fold or tear cards into geometric shapes or snowflakes. Display the finished tree in some part of your church building or plan to donate it to a nursing home, a shut-in person, etc.

Holiday Service Project

Materials: Sugar cookies, frosting, plastic knives, cookie decorations, green construction paper, glitter glue, scissors, costumes for the Christmas story.

Procedure: Children plan and supervise a Christmas party for a younger group of children. Older children decorate cookies and cut out large construction paper Christmas trees for younger children to decorate. Children then choose parts, dress up and practice acting the Christmas story for their presentation to the younger children.

Christmas Crafts and Activities © 1998 by Gospel Light. Permission to photocopy granted.

Hanukkah Celebration

Materials: Books about Hanukkah, menorah, dreidels, latkes (or other Hanukkah treat) and juice.

Preparation: Familiarize yourself with the story of Hanukkah.

Procedure: Hold a Hanukkah celebration to introduce children to the historical meaning of the holiday and help them discover the significance these events can have for contemporary Christians. Serve special foods, hold a special candle-lighting service and read the story of Hanukkah. Display a menorah and let children spin dreidels.

Advent Celebration

Materials: Bible, Advent wreath and red candles, matches.

Procedure: Each week children light one of the red candles. Explain that the word "advent" means "coming" or "arrival." **As we light each candle in the weeks prior to Christmas, we look forward to celebrating the birth of the Lord Jesus Christ.** Use the following theme ideas for each week:

Week 1—Good News Candle. Explain that the prophets told the good news of the coming of Jesus. **The Bible is good news telling us of God and His love for us.** Read Isaiah 9:6.

Week 2—Hope Candle. **Jesus gave hope to people that God still loved and cared for them. The angels told the good news that Jesus had come.** Read Luke 2:8-11.

Week 3—Joy Candle. **When the shepherds heard the good news, they hurried to see Jesus. After they saw Him, they rejoiced and went to tell others.** Read Luke 2:15-20.

Week 4—Love Candle. **God shows us His love through Jesus Christ, His Son, and helps us to show love to others.** Read John 3:16.

Stories

Story Tips

Everyone loves to hear the story of Christmas! And these delightful installments written by Ethel Barrett simply demand to be read aloud. Each segment is full of captivating word pictures and dramatic action—just what children of all ages love! To convey the full feeling and charm of these stories, practice reading the stories ahead of time. The following tips will help you read the stories with more confidence and greater effect:

- Use your normal speaking voice. Read clearly, distinctly and slowly, but avoid the tones and mannerisms people often adopt when talking to someone they think cannot hear or understand.
- Try whispering when you come to a crucial point in the narrative. A whisper is the most dramatic sound the human voice can utter.
- Vary your speaking rate—speeding up or slowing down—in order to convey importance or secure attention. An occasional pause is very effective in creating suspense.
- Add sound effects where appropriate.

- Add gestures when they fit.
- Put yourself in the place of the characters and speak and act as they would. For example, stand in a regal pose when you speak as Herod and bow humbly when you speak as the shepherds.
- Use facial expressions to convey emotions. Smile when referring to good things. Look angry or frightened or sad when that is how a story character might have felt.

(Tips adapted from Gospel Light's *Everything You Want to Know About Teaching Young Children, Birth-6 Years*.)

The Greatest Promise in the World

Luke 1:26-38, Matthew 1:18-25

Once a long, long time ago, the greatest gift in the WORLD was promised. Can you imagine a gift so great and so important that it changed the whole world?

Well, there was a gift just that important. It was a gift God had promised to send to the world.

It wasn't a palace.

It wasn't gold.

It was A BABY! And it was a very special baby—God's own Son, the baby Jesus.

This gift was promised to a young woman named Mary and to a kind man named Joseph. And this is how it all happened.

Mary and Joseph lived in Bible times. One day Mary was praying to God. She didn't know there was going to be a gift. She didn't expect an angel. She didn't even expect a PROMISE. But SUDDENLY an angel appeared! Right there before her eyes!

Mary was frightened. She'd never SEEN an angel before. And this angel was SPEAKING to her!

"Don't be afraid, Mary," the angel said. "God loves you very much. You are going to be the mother of a dear baby boy. He'll be God's own Son. And His name will be Jesus."

And then the angel was gone—just like that!

Mary stayed there and thought and thought. *This was a most wonderful promise. GOD made this promise. And when GOD makes a promise, He always keeps it. Why, this would be the greatest gift in the world!*

Then one night while Joseph was sleeping, he saw an angel too! And the angel told him all about Mary and the wonderful promise.

Oh, joy!

I'm going to be the mother of a baby boy, Mary thought as she made some blankets to keep Him warm. *He will be God's Son,* she thought as she made clothes for Him to wear. *His name will be Jesus,* she thought as she fixed a bed for Him to sleep in.

So Mary and Joseph got ready for the wonderful gift, because they knew for certain it was coming. They had seen an ANGEL. God had promised the gift. And God always keeps His promises.

LET'S TALK ABOUT THE BIBLE STORY

Find these promises in the Bible: Genesis 28:15; Psalm 121:3; Isaiah 41:10; Jeremiah 33:3; Romans 8:28; Philippians 4:19. God's promise to send His Son was the most wonderful promise of all. Do you know why? (See John 3:16.) Aren't you glad God always keeps His promises? How can you thank Him for this?

Stories • **All Ages**

A BIBLE VERSE TO LEARN

Not one word has failed of all [God's] *good promises.* (I Kings 8:56)

LET'S TALK TO GOD

Dear God, we're certainly glad to know that when You make a promise You always keep it. Help us to remember this and to believe You. And help us to keep OUR promises, too! In Jesus name, Amen.

The Promise Comes True

Luke 2:1-7

God had made Mary and Joseph a promise. But it wasn't an ordinary promise; it was an EARTH-SHAKING promise. He promised them a very special baby—God's own Son, the baby Jesus.

Imagine!

Of course, Mary should have gone to the very best hospital or maybe even a king's palace for this very special baby to be born. Or she could have stayed home and had servants and nurses hurrying and scurrying about, carrying trays and orange juice and sheets and medicine and bumping into each other. Maids would have combed her hair and bathed the new baby and dressed him in the finest clothing and brushed what little hair he had up to a curl on top and carried him to her bedside and put him gently alongside her, with his tiny head snuggled in the pillow.

But none of this happened at all.

What really happened is quite amazing.

It all began with an emperor's order. The Bible tells us that Caesar Augustus, the Roman emperor, decided that everyone in the world had to be counted, so that everyone could be taxed. This meant that Joseph and Mary had to pack a few belongings on a little donkey, leave their comfortable little house in Nazareth and clump along bumpy roads all the way to Bethlehem (Joseph's hometown)—just to be counted and to pay their taxes!

Then there was the matter of the crowds. When Joseph and Mary finally got to Bethlehem, it was just SPILLING OVER with other people who had also come to pay their taxes—people and donkeys and camels and bundles and food and sheep and goats. You just can't IMAGINE the confusion!

And then there was the matter of a place to stay. And THAT was the worst part, because there WAS no place to stay. The inns, which were like hotels, only instead of having cars the people had donkeys and camels to park out in a stable, were filled. EVERY place that had rooms to rent was filled. And poor Mary and Joseph went all over Bethlehem, knocking on doors and getting turned away and knocking on doors and getting turned away.

Finally one innkeeper said, "Wait!" He had just thought of something. And what he thought of was not a room with nice beds and clean sheets and a warm bath. It was a STABLE—where the donkeys and camels and sheep and cows slept! But that is where Mary and Joseph went to spend the night. And that was where, that very night, God's promise came true—the baby Jesus was

Stories • **All Ages**

born. Instead of a bed with clean sheets, there was straw; and instead of servants, nurses and doctors, there were donkeys, camels, sheep and cows to watch over Mary, Joseph and baby Jesus.

Yes, there baby Jesus was born. And there, Mary wrapped Him in soft clean cloth and laid Him—oh, so carefully—on some clean straw in a manger, a feedbox for animals.

It might SEEM that everything had gone wrong. But, actually, everything had gone exactly as God wanted it to go.

Jesus had been promised. And now He was HERE!

LET'S TALK ABOUT THE BIBLE STORY

Just imagine how different the world would be if God hadn't kept His promise. Can you think of some ways in which it would be different? Can you think of some ways you can thank God for keeping this great promise?

A BIBLE VERSE TO LEARN

[God] *loved us and sent his Son.*
(1 John 4:10)

LET'S TALK TO GOD

Dear God, we thank You that You loved us so much that You sent us the Lord Jesus to be our Savior. It sure was a great promise and we're glad You kept it. In Jesus' name, Amen.

The Strangest Announcement in the World

Luke 2:8-20

When new babies are born, how do people find out about it? On the phone? In an e-mail message? In an announcement card? In a letter? Do people call it out from their front porch? Clearly, the very FIRST thing to do is to let everybody know, one way or the other, as soon as possible!

"A baby!"

"Really?"

"Yes—a boy!"

"How big?"

"Eight and a half pounds!?"

"My, a BIG fellow! How wonderful!"

It's just too important to keep secret!

When Jesus was born, there were no announcement cards sent out; and in Bible times there were no phones or computers. But people still found out about it—in the strangest ways!

Some people who found out about it lived nearby. They were shepherds. They found out about it in the middle of the night. And this is how it happened.

The shepherds were watching their sheep in nearby fields. Everything was so quiet they could hear a blade of grass if it twittered in the breeze. Once in a while, a baby lamb would wake up and go "Baaaaa," but its mother would lick its ears and say "Shhhhhhhh," and it would go back to sleep. Then everything would be quiet again.

Then SUDDENLY, there was an ANGEL—right before their eyes! And a bright, BRIGHT light—right in the sky!

The shepherds couldn't believe their eyes. They looked at the angel. And at the bright light. And at each other. And they were afraid.

"Don't be afraid," the angel said. "I have good news! A Savior, Christ Jesus, has just been born. He is in Bethlehem right this minute. Lying in a manger."

The Savior! Oh, joy! Could it be TRUE?! the shepherds thought.

Just then the sky was FULL of angels. And they were saying, "Glory to God in the highest, and on earth peace and good will toward people." Then, suddenly, the angels were gone. And the bright light was gone. And it was dark again.

The shepherds looked at each other. *It MUST be true!* they thought. They would GO to Bethlehem and see what had happened. And they DID.

They ran across the fields and down the road to Bethlehem. They ran through the

streets, looking and searching everywhere.

Then they came to a stable. They looked in the doorway. There was Mary. There was Joseph. There were sheep. There were donkeys and camels and cows. There was a manger with straw in it. And there—all snuggled in the straw—was baby Jesus!

It was true!

"Shhhh." They quietly went in. And "Shhh." They slowly knelt down. And "Shhh." They thanked God for baby Jesus.

And then they went and told what they had seen to everyone they could find.

Oh, the shepherds were so happy! For they had found out about the most important baby that has ever been born. Not from a telephone call. Not from an announcement card. Not from a letter. But from ANGELS and a light in the sky!

The angels and the bright light announced that this was not just ANY baby—this was God's Son.

LET'S TALK ABOUT THE BIBLE STORY

Can you think of other ways God might have announced that Jesus was born? Why do you suppose God chose this way? How can you help other people know the good news that God sent His Son to be our Savior?

A BIBLE VERSE TO LEARN

Today in the town of David [Bethlehem] *a Savior has been born to you; he is Christ the Lord.* (Luke 2:11)

LET'S TALK TO GOD

Dear God, first You made a promise and then You kept it and then You TOLD people about it. We certainly thank You for all this. Help us to remember that it's important to tell people about that promise and all about how You kept it by sending your Son. In Jesus' name, Amen.

Two Dreams That Saved a Little Child

Matthew 2:1-15

People found out about the birth of Jesus in some very strange ways. There were shepherds who lived nearby who found out about it. And there were people who lived far away who found out about it. They were called wise men. And when THEY found out about it, they did something that nearly caused baby Jesus harm—DREADFUL harm. It happened this way.

These wise men studied the stars. They knew that God had promised to send a Savior-King. One night they saw a HUGE star, brighter than all the rest. And they knew it must be the star that would lead them to the Savior-King, Jesus.

So they packed some gifts and got on their camels and followed that star right to Jerusalem. And they went straight to the palace where King Herod lived.

"We have followed God's star," they told King Herod. "We are looking for the new King God promised."

King Herod was very polite and asked them all about the star. Then King Herod said to the wise men, "The child is not here; but when you find Him, let me know where He is. I would like to worship Him, too." And he sent them on their way.

The wise men left the palace and went to look for Jesus. But they didn't know one thing: Herod was a WICKED king. And he didn't want to find Jesus to WORSHIP Him. He wanted to KILL Him!

When the wise men came to where Mary and Joseph and little Jesus were, they unpacked their camels and brought out the finest gifts of gold and rare perfumes. And they knelt down and worshiped Jesus. Then they got ready to go back and tell King Herod where Jesus was. And they would have told him, and Jesus might have been KILLED—except for one thing: God was watching!

That night in a dream, God told the wise men, "Do not go back to wicked King Herod. He doesn't want to worship Jesus. He wants to have Him KILLED. Go back to your own country!"

And the wise men did!

King Herod was very angry. He called his soldiers. "Go to Bethlehem," he told them, "and find this child. I want to have Him killed!"

But God was still watching!

In a dream, God told Joseph to take Mary and Jesus and run away. Mary and Joseph packed their things, wrapped up little Jesus and stole out of the city and across the desert until they got to Egypt, a country far away.

When the soldiers got to Bethlehem and looked in all the places where there were little children so they could kill baby Jesus, He was gone!

King Herod never found Jesus. And Mary and Joseph didn't bring Him back until the wicked king was dead. No harm had come to God's Son, because God was watching!

LET'S TALK ABOUT THE BIBLE STORY

Phew! That was close, wasn't it? They didn't have e-mail and phones back in Bible times, but God used other ways to announce Jesus' birth and other ways to SAVE Jesus when His life was in danger. What were they? What are some ways God protects YOU from danger?

A BIBLE VERSE TO LEARN

The Lord will keep you from all harm.
(Psalm 121:7)

LET'S TALK TO GOD

Dear God, we thank You for taking such good care of Jesus and for letting the wise men know about Him, and then we thank You ESPECIALLY for not letting that wicked King Herod go and spoil it all. We thank You for giving us parents and teachers and policemen and all sorts of people to keep us safe. In Jesus' name, Amen.

Snacks

Snack Tips

Give kids a sample of the delicious, never-to-be-forgotten tastes of Christmas! In addition to keeping kids' faces smiling and their tummies full, snacks can also provide an enriching learning experience; kids get a chance to learn coopera- 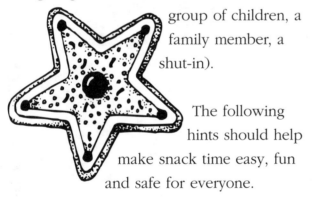 tion, sharing and how things are measured and food is actually prepared. Many of the recipes can be used to help kids experience the real joy of Christmas—preparing something to give to someone else (another group of children, a family member, a shut-in).

The following hints should help make snack time easy, fun and safe for everyone.

Preparation and Organization Tips

When planning to cook, preparation and organization are very important. Before you try recipes that require extensive measuring, it's wise to provide several measuring experiences, showing the children the correct way to use both dry and liquid measuring utensils.

- Provide a comfortable working space that is child-sized.
- Gather and set out ingredients and equipment before children begin.
- Read through the recipe together.
- Go over safety rules together.
- Clean up as you go along.

Safety and Health Tips

- Always wash hands before handling food.
- Things that are hot don't always look hot. If someone gets burned, immediately hold the burned area under cold running water.
- When chopping, cutting or peeling food, use a cutting board.
- Keep pot handles on the stove turned away from you.
- Turn the burner or oven off before removing pans.
- Stand mixing bowls in the sink as you stir to avoid splashes.

- Use hand beaters, a large spoon or a wire whip instead of electric beaters. This way, children have a chance to get the feel of the batter.
- Demonstrate and let children practice using utensils.
- Store sharp utensils out of children's reach.
- Keep hands dry while working in the kitchen. Wet, slippery hands can cause spills and accidents.
- Keep pot holders dry. If damp, they will absorb heat and lead to burns.

- When cutting with a knife, always cut away from yourself and keep fingers away from the blade.
- To help prevent steam burns, tip the lid away from you whenever you raise the cover of a hot pan.
- Electrical appliances should be used by ADULTS ONLY.
- Young children should not use the stove at all.
- Make sure hot foods are thoroughly cooked and any leftovers are quickly refrigerated.
- Instruct children in advance how to deal with a sneeze or a cough.

(These helpful cooking tips are from *The Big Book of Theme Parties, Snacks and Games* by Gospel Light.)

Super-Rich Hot Chocolate Mix

Materials: 1-pound can of instant chocolate powdered drink mix, 7-ounce jar of powdered creamer, 10 2/3 cups powdered milk, 1 1/2 cups powdered sugar, large mixing bowl, mixing spoon, measuring cups, teaspoon, water, hot plate or microwave oven, container in which to boil water, one mug for each child. Yield: over one gallon.

Procedure: Bring water to a boil. Children measure, mix and stir all dry ingredients in a bowl. Pour 3 heaping teaspoons of mixed ingredients into each mug. Fill each mug with boiling water. Stir thoroughly and serve. (Or mix one rounded cup of mixture into 5 cups of hot water and pour into separate mugs.)

Peanut Butter and Chocolate Cookies

Materials: 2 cups sugar, 1/2 cup milk, 1/4 cup cocoa, 3 cups rolled oats, 1/4 pound (one stick) butter or margarine, 1/2 cup peanut butter, 1 teaspoon vanilla, measuring cups and spoons, saucepan, mixing spoon, hot plate, waxed paper, serving plate. Yield: approximately two dozen small cookies.

Procedure: In saucepan, combine milk, sugar and cocoa. Boil for one minute. Remove from heat and stir in all other ingredients. Drop by spoonfuls onto waxed paper. When dough is slightly cooled, use hands to mold dough into balls. When cookie balls have hardened, put on plate to serve.

Christmas Sugar Cookies

Materials: Several dozen sugar cookies, frosting, red and green food coloring, several small plastic bowls with lids, spoon, plastic sandwich bags, scissors, Christmas napkins; optional—green or red yarn or narrow ribbon.

Preparation: Beforehand, make several dozen cookies, using your favorite sugar cookie recipe or refrigerated sugar cookie dough from the grocery store. Use cookie cutters to make Christmas shapes such as bells and stars. Make your favorite frosting recipe or purchase 3 cans of ready-made white frosting. Color 1/3 of the frosting green and 1/3 red. Put small amounts of each color of frosting in individual plastic bags. Roll top of each bag over so that frosting won't leak out the top. Cut a small tip off a bottom corner of each bag to make it into a "pastry decorator." Carefully set each bag on its side on a napkin so frosting doesn't leak out the corner.

Procedure: Children squeeze the bags to decorate their cookies with frosting. After first layer of frosting dries, children may add other decorative details. Serve cookies, using Christmas napkins. (Optional: Put extra cookies in unused plastic bags, tie with yarn or ribbon and give to children as gifts to take home.)

Kabobs for Kids

Materials: Plastic knives, red and green finger gelatin (see recipes below), miniature marshmallows, sandwich picks, fruit (apples, oranges, pineapple chunks, bananas), lemon juice, large paper plates.

Preparation: Follow these recipes to make red and green finger gelatin—a unique treat firm enough to be picked up using fingers.

RED GELATIN

2 cups cranberry juice

3 envelopes unflavored gelatin

Soften gelatin in 1/2 cup cranberry juice. Bring 1 1/2 cups cranberry juice to a boil. Add hot juice to softened gelatin mixture and stir until gelatin is completely dissolved. Pour into a 9x13-inch (22.5x32.5-cm) pan and chill until firm. Makes about 60 3/4-inch (1.9-cm) squares.

GREEN GELATIN

6-ounce can of apple juice concentrate

3 envelopes unflavored gelatin

1 1/2 cups boiling water

green food coloring

Soften gelatin in apple juice concentrate. Add 1 1/2 cups boiling water and a few drops of green food coloring. Stir until gelatin is completely dissolved. Pour into a 9x13-inch (22.5x32.5-cm) pan and chill until firm. Makes about 60 3/4-inch (1.9-cm) squares.

Procedure: Have children cut red and green finger gelatin into approximately 3/4-inch (1.9-cm) cubes. Children alternate gelatin cubes with miniature marshmallows on sandwich picks. Then they cut fruit into snack-sized pieces and alternate different fruit pieces on other sandwich picks. (Sprinkle lemon juice on the fruit kabobs to keep fruit from turning brown.) Children alternate gelatin kabobs and fruit kabobs on large paper plates to form a wheel design.

Banana Snowballs

Materials: Lemon juice, custard-style vanilla yogurt, several small bowls or containers, flaked coconut, spoon, bananas, knife, cutting board, plastic forks, plate; optional—red and/or green food coloring.

Preparation: Pour lemon juice and yogurt into several separate containers. Place coconut in separate bowl. (Optional: Color coconut with food coloring.)

Procedure: Stir yogurt well. Cut peeled bananas into 1-inch (2.5-cm) pieces. Spear banana piece on fork, dip in lemon juice and then in yogurt (make sure it's coated), roll in coconut and place on plate. When all banana pieces have been coated, sit down and enjoy the treat!

Haystacks

Materials: 1 pound white chocolate, 2 cups pretzel sticks (broken), 1 1/2 cups peanuts (salted or unsalted), container in which to melt chocolate (double boiler or microwave-safe dish), hot plate or microwave oven, tablespoon, waxed paper, plate; optional—red or green food coloring.

Procedure: Help children melt chocolate. (Optional: Add food coloring). Add pretzels and peanuts. Stir until well coated. Drop by tablespoonfuls onto waxed paper. When hardened, put on plate. Yield: approximately 2 dozen.

Alternate idea: Dip pretzels into melted chocolate and set on waxed paper to harden.

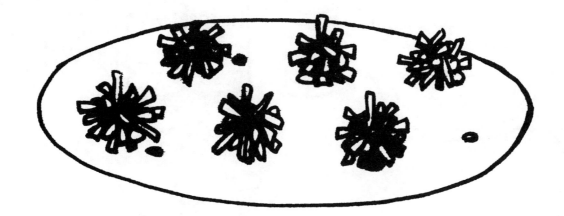

Festive Punch

Materials: 3 large cans or jars of red fruit juice (tropical punch, strawberry juice, etc.), 2 quarts of ginger ale, large punch bowl, ice cubes, 2 boxes of thawed frozen strawberries, mixing spoon, ladle, cups; optional—pint of lime sherbet.

Procedure: Mix fruit juice and ginger ale in large punch bowl. Add ice cubes and strawberries. Stir thoroughly and serve in cups. (Optional: Spoon green sherbet to float in the red punch just before serving.)

Birthday Sundae

Materials: Vanilla frozen yogurt, several dessert toppings (fresh fruits, granola, raisins, etc.), bowls, plastic knives, cutting board, spoons, paper cups, napkins; optional—party decorations (balloons, streamers, etc.), Christmas decorations (nativity scene, greenery, bows, etc.), birthday cake or cupcakes, Christmas music.

Procedure: Children prepare the toppings for frozen yogurt sundaes: cut fruit, place toppings in separate bowls and set out spoons and napkins.

Invite children to pray with you, thanking God for sending Jesus to earth. Volunteers complete the sentence, "Dear Jesus, thank You for...." Children spoon frozen yogurt into cups and add toppings. (Optional: Divide children into two groups. One group decorates the room with party decorations you have provided, while the other group prepares the sundaes. Encourage children to sing "Happy Birthday" to Jesus.)

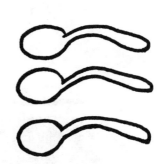

Finger Gelatin

Materials: Ingredients for finger gelatin (see "Preparation" below), 9×13-inch (22.5×32.5-cm) pan, metal spatula, seasonal cookie cutters (bells, stars, trees, etc.), paper plates, napkins.

Preparation: For every 12 children, prepare one pan of finger gelatin. Dissolve 4 envelopes of unflavored gelatin in 1 cup cold water. Dissolve 1 6-ounce package of red (or green) gelatin and 1 3-ounce package of lemon gelatin in 4 cups boiling water. Then mix the two gelatin mixtures together and pour into pan. (Pan does not need to be coated; shapes can be easily removed with metal spatula.) Refrigerate until firm. (Once gelatin is firm, refrigeration is not needed.)

Procedure: Help children take turns cutting gelatin shapes with cookie cutters and then removing shapes from pan onto paper plates. Use the shapes as a way to talk with children about the good news of Jesus' birth.

Cookie Toppers

Materials: Prepared vanilla frosting (a lower-sugar alternative to frosting: add a little honey to cream cheese and whip with an electric mixer), two bowls, red and green food coloring, two mixing spoons, sturdy plain cookies, plastic knives; optional—a variety of toppings (candy sprinkles, coconut, crushed nuts, etc.).

Procedure: Divide frosting into two bowls. Children mix food coloring into frosting and then frost cookies to share among themselves or with others. (Optional: Children sprinkle toppings onto frosting.)

Edible Nativity

Materials: Aluminum foil, 9x12-inch (22.5x30-cm) piece of cardboard, frosting, graham crackers, pretzel sticks, miniature marshmallows, toothpicks, animal crackers, shredded wheat biscuits, other food decorations (dry cereal, chocolate stars, candy sprinkles, etc.).

Preparation: Cover cardboard with foil. Spread frosting onto the foil-covered cardboard.

Procedure: Children use graham crackers and/or pretzel sticks to form sides of stable and manger on frosting-covered cardboard base. People and animals may be made from marshmallows, toothpicks and pretzel sticks; or, for animals, use animal crackers. Crumble shredded wheat biscuits to create hay. Use other food decorations to decorate the nativity scene.

Marshmallow Snowflakes

Materials: Regular and miniature marshmallows, toothpicks, bamboo skewers, paper plates.

Procedure: Working on paper plates, children make edible snowflakes by connecting regular and miniature marshmallows with toothpicks and bamboo skewers. When snowflakes are completed, children show their creations to group before the snowflakes are taken apart and eaten (or taken home).

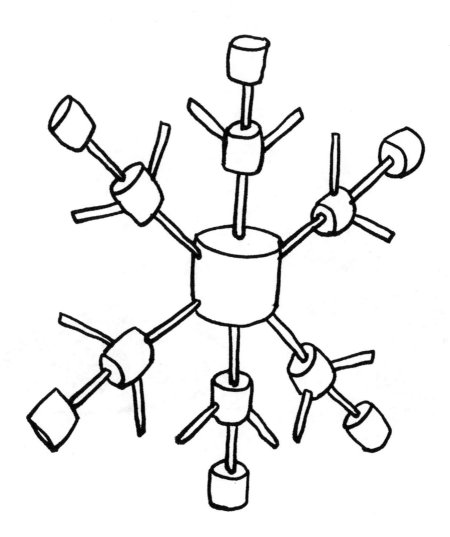

Oatmeal Fudge

Materials: Hot plate, stove or microwave oven, sauce pan, double boiler or microwave-safe bowl, measuring utensils, spoon, white and brown sugars, milk, butter, white corn syrup, chunky peanut butter, chocolate chips, oatmeal, large pan, knife, paper plates.

Procedure: In a saucepan or double boiler mix 1 cup white sugar, 1 cup brown sugar, 1/2 cup and 2 tablespoons milk, 1/4 cup butter and 3 tablespoons white corn syrup. Bring to a boil slowly. Boil one minute and remove from heat then add 1/2 cup chunky peanut butter and 2 cups chocolate chips. Stir until well blended. Stir in 3 cups oatmeal. Spread in large pan and let set for several hours. Cut into 1 1/2-inch (3.75-cm) squares and serve on plates.

Roll, Cut and Bake Sugar Cookies

Materials: A package of refrigerated sugar cookie dough, Christmas cookie cutters, rolling pin, waxed paper, toaster oven, small cookie sheet, spatula, paper plates.

Procedure: Children cut shapes from dough that has been rolled on waxed paper. Bake cookies in toaster oven as directed on package. Children share cookies with each other.